D1450597

Trouble Is a Gift

Jim in uniform 1951

Trouble Is a Gift

A Story of Addiction, Recovery, and Hope

James S. Cusack

S and J Publishing
Kerhonkson, New York

Printed in the United States of America.
Book and cover design by Bill McAllister.

S and J Publishing
5 Ridgeview Road
P.O.Box 610
Kerhonkson, New York 12446

Distributed by Epigraph Publishing Service
Hardcover: ISBN 978-1-936940-49-3

Library of Congress Control Number: Available from publisher

CONTENTS

Acknowledgments

It is with a deep sense of appreciation that I humbly thank the thousands of people I've met during my lifetime who inspired me and helped me write my story.

I'm particularly grateful to my mother and father for their unceasing prayers, rosaries, holy water, and novenas, who never gave up on me; my sister-in-law Elaine and my brother Jack; Tom Lavery, designated driver and guardian angel; all their children and grandchildren.

To my wife's family: her sister, Joan, and brother-in-law, Steve Lewis; all their children and grandchildren; her brother, Jimmy Boylston, killed by a drunk driver in 1971; and his wife, Maureen.

To ALL our nieces, nephews, grandnieces, and grandnephews mentioned above, whom we love dearly and have been the children we never had.

To my sponsor, Joe Lemmon, truly a saint who never gave up on me.

To my Middletown family, Millie and children.

To my Glen Acre Lodge family, Doris and my much loved stepchildren, Margie, Bobby, Pat, and Elaine.

To all my colleagues in the chemical dependency treatment field, especially Monsignor Joseph Dunne who was so instrumental in my beginning and remaining in the field, for their support and willingness to exchange information and findings generously and freely so we can all benefit.

To the editors and writers at Epigraph Publishing Service and the Villa, I extend thanks and appreciation for your expertise and patience with rewrites, extended deadlines, and t-crossings and i-dottings that brought this book to its logical conclusion.

Finally, to my wife of forty years, Sue, the love of my life, my best friend, my business partner: my forever gratitude for the way you have changed my life and taught me to be proud enough of myself and our mission to have the courage to complete this book.

With love and appreciation always,

Jim

Preface

The reason I am writing this book is to share the blessings I have received and have tried to incorporate into my recovery with the hope it will offer help and hope to others.

I am going to be eighty-four years old this coming April 26th, 2013, and have sixty years of sobriety. It has been quite a journey, filled with a lifetime of both joys and sorrows. The message I would like to give through this book is to realize that one can benefit from the experiences of other people—that hurts, disappointments, and disillusionments can lead to a new way of life. To realize that trouble IS a gift. Hope comes from the sharing and understanding with others.

One major message I would like to share is something that has and still means the world to me: it is in the giving that we receive.

Introduction

My name is Jim Cusack, and I'm an alcoholic. By the end of this story you'll know that in the year 2013, I'm eighty-three years of age and I've been blessed with sixty consecutive years of sobriety. My goal is to pass along my "experience, strength, and hope" so these might do others some good. How? Well, to see the process of recovery from alcoholism and chemical dependency in a different light from that supplied by PhDs and their dissertations on the subject. A lot of the old-timers stressed simplicity in recovery. But those guys I looked up to in the early days are all gone. And now—surprise, surprise—I'm the old-timer. Helping people find sobriety has been my mission in life.

My own story gets pretty dark. That's nothing new to the disease of alcoholism. But the history of the road that opened up under my feet after I came through the fire is really the history of recovery. And hopefully, that may be of interest to some of you.

A lot of times in pages to come you'll hear me say "in the rooms." That's when I'm talking about Twelve-Step meetings. Indeed, in the rooms you'll often hear it said, "I came here for my drinking and I stayed for my thinking." In other words: You come in to save your life. Because if you keep drinking, you're as good as dead—and in the back of your mind, you know that. Maybe it's in the front of your mind, by now. Or written all over every inch of you. So you come in to survive, and then along the way, though you weren't looking for it and you thought those people talking about it were nuts, you find a serenity you never dreamed of together with a contentment, fulfillment, and at times—for a kicker—even happiness.

ONE

Beginnings

TODAY I REALIZE I was born the alcoholic son of immigrant parents from County Clare, in Ireland, who came to this country, like a few hundred thousand other starving Irish men, women, and children, to escape the potato famines of the 1920s. Maybe you know the Irish were looked down on back then. And that we fought our way up, and no, it wasn't always pretty. The people I grew up around, like most of the Irish immigrants, were known as hard workers who didn't complain about the cold or how heavy a load was. The Irish took jobs no one else wanted because the truth is these were the only jobs we could get—on the docks, in the quarries, shoveling ditches, washing dishes, sweeping streets, fighting and clawing our way up to a certain level of decency. Most of us were Irish Catholics. A God-fearing lot.

I was born in 1929 on 100th Street and Amsterdam Avenue; but my first memories begin at 124th Street and Morningside Avenue in Harlem, where we moved when I was two. It was here my family lived until I was ten or eleven. We were only four of us, my older brother, Jack, my parents, and me, which was a pretty small number for an Irish family back then.

My father was in the Teamsters Union working in warehousing and trucking. Out of the eight sons born to his parents, Pop was the only relatively sober one in the lot. I couldn't say about his three sisters. Pop would have one or two drinks once in a while. Maybe a couple of times a year he'd get drunk and my mother would have it out with him. The truth is, he brought the money home without stopping off at the bar, which was a rare thing where I grew up. Not that he had some uppity attitude about it, though maybe my mother did. Me, on the other hand, I took after my uncles. When I was four or so, there was a family wedding where I went around with a cousin finishing all these different drinks. Of course, we were blotto in no time. Soon everybody in the family was laughing at us, these little clowns, staggering around, draining glasses, until I fell asleep on a pile of coats and didn't remember the drive home.

Maybe my mother took to watching me more closely, for all the good it did. Still, I got a hot toddy with whiskey of some kind in it whenever I was sick. And I liked that fine. I also liked taking my castor oil because I could usually get a shot of something in that, too. So did I have a predisposition to alcohol? You bet. I was already exhibiting basic alcoholic behaviors before the age of ten.

Indeed, there was a "County" mentality in those days back in the old Irish pocket of Harlem. People from Clare and other parts of the old country rallied together. We watched each other's backs. Families looked in on each other in the good times and bad. And even though I didn't have a dozen brothers and sisters, I almost felt like I did—because everywhere I went I knew everyone, and they called my name as I went by. I was basically a good kid, though my parents told me I was stubborn.

I remember one incident in particular. Maybe I was five, I can't say for sure. I walked into the house one day wearing my coat. I took it off, threw it on the floor, and I wouldn't pick it up. Guess I was pissed off about something. Now, my parents didn't go for this kind of thing. They yelled in my face and I soon took a bit of a beating. Honestly, they seemed more upset than me, but I dug in my heels and for whatever reason, I wouldn't pick up that coat. I'm mentioning this now because I believe that some if not most individuals who grow up to become alcoholics and addicts are born a little different from other people. They react differently. And as they get older, they handle their drug of choice differently from people who don't become addicted. It becomes a shield for them, some kind of invisible protection supplying them with a magical power. This can escalate until they feel like superheros when they're using, people with some sort of secret identity, like other people might go through a phase as kids of having imaginary friends they share their hopes and fears with. Addicts and alcoholics start to live in a fantasy world which is only slightly removed from the real one. And guess what pushes it away from the real one? That's right. Their drug of choice.

My knuckles had scabs on them most of the time because, growing up in Harlem, I came up tough pretty quick. I wasn't the biggest kid, so I was tough from the start. I made a name for myself and I fought to keep it. Even as a youngster I had this sort of fearless reputation. It got to the point where I'd intentionally go outside the neighborhood to make trouble. And it wasn't hard to do in those days. You just looked at a kid from another neighborhood a second longer than you should and it all started to boil. If you didn't look away, there would be words. Then if you didn't back down, there would be action. I fought kids my own age and I fought kids bigger than me. I liked the challenge. Why? Well, there are a couple of ways to look at it. From a chemical point of view, you realize the adrenalin is pumping like crazy, and sure enough, you're high on it. Like on a drug. From the self-esteem angle, you want to be somebody, somebody special who commands respect, maybe even a touch of awe. These days you get that by being a movie star or a pop singer. But there are still parts of the world where you can only get that by being a gangster or a dealer. Back then, for an Irish kid like me, the only way you could inspire awe was by being a tough guy.

It all started to get real for me when I saw my father get in a fist fight. What an unforgettable impression it left on me! For starters, a bunch of us kids used to box on Friday nights. Some of the older guys like "Pete Cowboy," who was about eighteen or nineteen at the time, used to egg me on. They'd call me "Apple Eyes," which really got my goat. It would probably make me smile today if someone called me "Apple Eyes" because it would mean I was talking to a survivor from a lost world, but back then I considered it a put-down which bothered me plenty. Anyway, this older kid "Pete Cowboy" was the local kingpin in the neighborhood. I don't think he really got involved in big stuff, no robberies or the like, but small-time trouble. Pete was tough and he was connected.

My father was a hard-working guy who, as I said, stayed out of trouble for the most part. I remember my mother caught him flirting with a woman one time and really boxed his ears. But basically he was one of those guys who plugged away at life without complaining. Soon he got higher up into the Teamsters and gained some notoriety there, but to tell you the truth, I was more impressed with my uncles who were the hell-raisers. But all that changed on a particular Saturday.

I was taking one of those old wooden slotted boxes filled with empty beer bottles to the corner store. We kids used to collect empties around the neighborhood and get two cents for every bottle—twenty-four bottles in a box, that's forty-eight cents—enough to buy a half-gallon of milk *and* a loaf of bread and maybe some cheese besides. Or the price of a quart of beer, if somebody would buy it for you and not snitch. But my mother knew about the empties and always wanted to see the money. Anyway, I'm on my way to the store with a full box when I see Pete Cowboy coming towards me on the sidewalk. So I raise my chin with a jerk the way tough kids do and mumble,

"Hey, Pete. How you doin'?" It wasn't a real question, mind you. You weren't really asking somebody how they were doing when you said that. In fact, you were sort of surprised as hell when some wiseguy actually tells you how he's doing when you ask him "How you doin'?" So naturally, Pete, being the tough guy he is, doesn't answer the question, but instead says, "What you got there, Apple Eyes?" And stops in front of me, blocking my way.

So I say, "You know damn well what I got here, Pete. What's it to you?"

He smiles and says, "It's a sin to say that terrible word, Cusack. Tell you what. I'll cash in the bottles for you and give the money to the sisters so your soul don't burn in hell."

"Nuts to that!" I say and try to move around him on the sidewalk. But he's bigger and stronger than me, and in a second he's wrestled the box out of my hands and shoved me against the building, raking his shoe down the instep of my right ankle to let me know he means business. So we exchange dirty looks, and I know the box is as good as gone—and the money too. And that's when I hear a shout that sounds vaguely familiar. He looks around and starts hustling with the box towards the alley. Then we hear the shout again, and I look, and it's my old man, running towards us. Tell you the truth, I don't know if I'd ever actually seen my father run before. It was kind of an astonishing sight. And there were all these jumbled up feelings in my chest, like I was glad Pop had seen it all, so I wouldn't be in trouble at home, but I'm in a daze. I figure my father will stop and make sure I'm all right. But I still can't help but feel like I did something wrong because, well, I usually do, and I usually get in trouble for it. But now Pete disappears down the alley. Pop doesn't hardly look at me but takes off after Pete. So I'm shocked. I mean—there's a part of me that's proud of him and all, for chasing after Pete. I'm thinking, if he catches up with him, Pete will beat him senseless. And then—I'm ashamed to admit to this, but honestly, what went through my head is that when Pete beats up my father, my mother will blame me, and I'll catch hell and be a laughingstock among the tough guys of the neighborhood. It's amazing how many thoughts can race through your brain in a second. But that's all in my head. Here on the street, I'm chasing after my father who's chasing after Pete, yelling, "Stop, thief!" Pete throws the box of empties onto a couple of garbage cans and turns to face my old man with one pissed-off look on his face. He puts up his fists and steps towards my old man, throwing one of those lefts to kind of set up a real punch. But Pop doesn't wait. He dodges the set up punch and flies at Pete with a right to the kisser followed with a fast left uppercut to the jaw—and it's goodnight, Irene. Pete goes down, and Pop might have even kicked him once in the ribs, I don't know—but it was like something I'd never seen, a part of him I didn't even know existed. To be truthful, I couldn't believe what was happening. He was standing over Pete yelling, "Get up, ya punk. I'll teach you to steal from my Jimmy! Get up! You big puffball, ya! Get up, I say!"

"It's okay, Pop. We got the bottles. You showed him, Pop. You showed him! Boy, oh boy, did you ever."

Now my father turns to me and this look of contorted rage just sort of melts into a joy-filled smile of love. I don't know, I guess he must have seen how proud I was of him. So he ruffles my hair and he says, "Jimmy, pick up your bottles there, son. And if you want to spit on that bit of scum, you go right ahead."

But this was Pete Cowboy Pop was talking about! And it was like suddenly I realized my father was the bravest guy on Earth. Well, I was too shocked to say another word. I just kind of picked up my bottles and stood staring in disbelief as Pete gathered himself up into a crouch and wiped the blood from his lip, staring at the back of his hand like he couldn't quite believe it either. He shoots one sort of shamefaced look my way, then he gets up and slinks down the alley, brushing himself off, without saying a word. He turns back once, rubbing his chin like he can't quite get over what hit him. Now windows are going up all down the alley, and people from the old country are shouting Pop's name and cheering us. So now my old man turns to me and—well, we start to laugh. I think maybe it was the happiest moment I'd ever know with him. No, I don't think it, I know it was. Because in two minutes flat, he'd gone from being this general pain in my ass to—well, there's no other word for it, he was my hero. And he stayed my hero for quite a long time. And sure, that was great for us, father and son, but it sort of poured gasoline on my fighting. It was like Pop did the right thing, but I took the right thing and went to the wrong place with it. Like most everything else I did, I went overboard. And sure, that's another characteristic of the alcoholic personality: a strong tendency to go to extremes.

But—and this is the stuff that's hard to explain about violence and the huge shifts in emotion it brings up—the thing is, Pete actually went around a couple of days later and found my father, and I couldn't believe this when I heard it, but he apologized to him, man to man. I think they might have even had a drink together, with Pete buying, of course. Now I already told you Pete Cowboy was kind of the head guy around our area of Harlem, and sure enough, after that he and my father became pretty good friends. And I benefited from that friendship, without a doubt. I didn't do anything bad with Pete. I didn't steal or rob or anything with him, but I got close enough to realize that he was into stuff that was a little more serious than I thought. But he drew the line with me, told me he didn't want me following him into that life. That being a tough guy was one thing, but he wanted me to play it straight—not get in with the mob or into trouble with the law, but to keep my nose clean. That was a very significant thing for me, and I still remember the whole situation very clearly. Pop's reputation in the neighborhood grew after punching out Pete Cowboy, what with them becoming friends afterwards. Funny, how this stuff happens. I don't know much about how the mob fit in with the Teamsters, except that back then they did somehow. So now people are tapping Pop on the shoulder, saying they want him to move up. But he won't go past the neighborhood. That's another story. The thing is—I have this picture of him as a tough guy now, but one of the guys in the white hats, if you know what I mean. Most kids don't see their old man beat up a kingpin; they don't see their father standing over a guy like that, yelling "Get up, ya punk!" and living to tell the tale. My father was defending his family and neighborhood, and he always stood up for what was right. The fact is, though I finally pulled my life together, there's a part of me that'll never feel the equal of my father. And towards the end of the game, I realize now, that's not such a terrible thing.

⚬⚬⚬

Like almost every Irish kid, I went to Catholic school, Saint Joseph's on 125th Street, where the nuns chased us around with rulers and told us we were going to burn in hell if we didn't do what they said. You've heard these kinds of stories before, about how usually very little of this early religion makes an actual impression on the likes of a little tough guy like me, which is what I was. But there was this one nun who was different from all the others. She had this glow about her—not an actual glow, but it was clear from looking at her that she was in this peaceful, happy relationship with God. And somehow we kids all kind of knew she was the real deal. And the higher-ups knew it too, which is why it was her job to tell us little kids about the life of Jesus for most of an hour every day.

That was a very special time, that hour, not that I would admit it; but I looked forward to it every day. And I wouldn't be surprised if some other little tough guys looked forward to it, too. Because she'd sit there with this unshakably sweet smile on her wrinkled, old face, and she'd tell us the story of Jesus. And I remember her looking me dead in the eye one time while saying to us, "He really lived, you know? He was a man, a carpenter who had to work for a living just like your fathers do. He went to the market and bought bread and food, just like your mothers do. He pumped water from a well into a jug and kept it by the kitchen door. And when he came home from work he washed his face and hands from the water in that jug, and poured some to drink into a cup. And then sat at the table and said his prayers and broke his bread, and then toddled off to bed tired from his day. He knelt before his bed and said his prayers to God, his Father in heaven. Just as we all do today. He really lived, this man we call Jesus. Don't forget that, ever."

I must have been . . . what? Eight years old? But I remember this like it was yesterday. It was like this shot of love went through me. Experiences like that make me say I was a complex kid, even though my speech was rough-and-tumble.

I have particularly fond memories of the day I made my First Holy Communion. It had a lot to do with that special nun with the glow about her. Because when I made my First Communion—it was as if I got some of that glow, too. Like this little Christmas tree bulb got lit up by God in my chest when I took the sacrament on my tongue and felt the priest's hand wave and make the cross over my head. Like I could feel this wind. And I looked over and saw my mother dabbing away the tears in her eyes, and my dad taking her hand and kissing it once. I don't think I ever saw him do a thing like that before or again. He was proud of me—and no, that didn't happen often. But he was proud. And I remember promising myself that I'd turn over a new leaf to keep them both proud of me. You know, stay out of trouble, buckle down, get all . . . Cs, anyway. But that didn't last long.

Truth is, I was a very mischievous kid, always looking to get into trouble, always looking for a fight. Nowadays, I look back and I can see the pathology. Like the sisters and priests would say of a troublemaker, "He's got the very divvel in him, he does!" But it was more that adrenalin from fighting and trouble, was this drug that lifted my feet off the ground. And I liked it up there. So without knowing it yet, I was chasing the buzz, even back then.

When I was eleven my family moved to Queens. At first, it was an awkward move. I'd established myself in Harlem, earned the respect of my peers. I was a leader of sorts, a tough kid who'd proved himself time and time again. People knew me to be smart, but at the same time I was a bit of a punk and a wiseguy. I had no fear. In Queens I had to rewrite my history, which meant I had to start from scratch. And that meant fighting.

Now, a big part of a fight takes place in the mind. For instance, if you're scared of a guy, chances are he's going to take you. After my father punched out Pete Cowboy, it became known around Harlem the Cusacks were tough. And I rode on the heels of that rep, and believe you me, that sort of stuff helps in a fight. But I didn't have those credentials in Queens, so it was almost like my punches didn't carry the same force. The guys weren't going down. More often it was me going down. Nothing was working for me, but I was too stubborn to take the hint. I went out to find more trouble. And in Queens, trouble was not hard to find.

My brother Jack left home to become a Christian Brother when I was eleven. As a result I grew up almost as an only child, but I liked that. I liked everything about it. I felt a new sense of adventure, knowing I'd have to reinvent myself on this new turf. I wasn't drinking on a daily basis yet, and the isolation didn't feel like loneliness yet. It made me feel different. In the rooms people will talk about alcoholism or addiction as if it has a personality of its own, like the big bad wolf disguised as your grandmother. Looking back at this time in my life, I get this creepy feeling. Even though I was only eleven. It's as if my disease knew I was isolated by being new, not having any siblings, and even more isolated for being fearless—a perfect situation for something evil to come up behind me. And lo and behold, that's exactly what happened.

Back then, I think I liked myself well enough. I knew I did wrong things at times, like smoking cigarettes and beating up punks; but just about every guy I knew was doing the same sort of stuff. I didn't think there was anything wrong with it. Oddly enough, this is exactly around the time I really started to get into trouble.

I started drinking wine regularly when I became an altar boy. Wine was kept in the sacristy, and every chance I got, I dipped into it. Back then my father got cigarettes by the carton. I'd open the carton, take a couple of packs, and reclose it. He never said anything about it to me and never told my mother. It was almost like a wink from him. They used to have weddings in the church on Saturdays, and I remember horsing around down there one Saturday afternoon and not remembering anything until the next morning. Early one Sunday my father woke me up and said, "What the hell did you do now? The pastor wants to see us down in the rectory." So down we went to the rectory, and sure enough the pastor was very upset. It seems this other guy and I had lit candles, and put one on every pew, and left the church. Thank God, we didn't burn the place down. But I had no recollection of lighting these candles whatsoever. At the time, I had no idea what a blackout was. I was literally clueless. Worse, I couldn't put two and two together. It was like a trick question. How do you remember not remembering? So after we got through with the chewing out from the pastor, I said to this kid who was with me, "Why did you tell him we did that?" Because I still didn't get the point that we *did* do this stuff but got too drunk to remember. So I asked him this, and he looked at me like I had two heads. Years later, when I finally started to sober up, I realized this is where I started to get spiritually wiped out. By which I mean, I'd always prided myself on taking the rap for whatever I'd done; but once I encountered this new animal in the zoo, this thing called a "blackout," well, my honor system went out the window. It wasn't long before I had no idea what I'd done the night before, and so there was no way to admit to it or apologize for it. It was like a monster was getting loose and ruining my reputation—a monster which pretty soon I would be calling my best friend. By the end of my drinking, my blackouts would last for a week, even two. By then I'd given up trying to figure out what I'd done. Instead, I just somehow found the money to continue the drunk so I wouldn't have to worry about anything until I "came to" again, which was for shorter and shorter periods of time. But that all came later.

When I graduated from grammar school, they tried talking me into becoming a priest, my mother mostly, but my father went along with it too, because he could see I was going downhill. Actually, for a minute or two—and this is the part that's hard to believe—it was *my* idea. And of course the priests pushed for it. Columban priests visited our school, like recruiters for the army do today. And they knew their job.

They were very convincing. So they "drafted" a bunch of us on the spot. Suddenly we all think we want to become priests. At first, I think it's a good idea to get away and join the clergy. You don't like the way your life is going? You have this secret little Christmas tree bulb from God lit in your wiseguy chest? So? You get this great idea. You think, "I'll go up to the country and change my life. I'll turn that little Christmas light into the tree at Rockefeller Center! Become a priest and turn myself into a legend, tough guy with a collar!" Of course, it didn't take me long to lose that idea. So it sounds crazy, I know—but we take a trip up to the Columban Fathers up in Silver Creek, New York. My parents drive me up with two other kids going for the same reason. But first, on our way up there, my parents decide to take a side trip to Niagara Falls. Now that was quite an experience in itself. Like nothing I'd ever seen before. This force of nature crashing down, the single most powerful thing God had made that any human being would ever see!

When we finally arrive at Silver Creek my parents get very involved with the Columban fathers and sisters, and they must have given them money and said a lot of prayers because I'm put in charge of the class—made the foreman, you might say; but that didn't last too long. Before three months is up I'm in deep trouble again. I know, this word "trouble" is getting to be like a refrain from a song. Believe me, if I could have changed myself into an angel back then, I would have. In fact, that's what I was up there trying to do.

I left the grounds a few times and wound up in a town called Dunkirk. The first time, the priests showed up in a station wagon to drive me back to seminary, but I had already gotten myself a few six packs, so at least I was properly bombed. I can't remember what the punishment was that time, but before you can say "Merry Christmas," I'm back into the sacristy with the wine. The priests are chastising me like crazy, always trying to straighten me out. So I "Yes, Father" them to death and just do as I like.

One of the guys I went up there with was deathly afraid of snakes. So I used to catch these garter snakes and put them in his desk. Luckily, the guy didn't have a heart attack. We were the best of friends, but I couldn't resist playing these jokes on him. Years later the same guy came into a detox I was running. Seems he'd been an altar boy who got into the wine, too! By then he was a former New York City cop. But I remember how terrified he was of the snakes I'd sneak into his desk. I regret such things now, but I didn't seem to think much of them then. And in years to come I'd behave in ways which lead me to believe I had no conscience—or that it had somehow been turned off. But at the time the question largest in my mind was: What was I thinking when I agreed to be a priest? I asked myself over and over. I didn't want to study or do chores. It got so bad I wasn't even saying the rosary like I would back at home as a bully with a religious streak. I lasted out the year, and the fathers told me that they didn't think I should come back, that I wasn't really priest material.

But I don't think it was a waste because I learned a few things. For instance, there was this farm we were supposed to help on. One time they slaughtered a pig and I didn't know what the hell to do with it. They had this pig hung up by its hind feet—already dead, but they slit open its guts and all its insides came bursting out, and it just seemed like the last thing in the world someone studying to be a priest should be involved with, sticking a pig with knives and all. But I was supposed to be a tough guy and know how to handle it. But I couldn't handle it, and I didn't want to be a priest anyway except for a moment there when maybe I did. It really shook me up to see the pig's blood busting out of its guts and bursting onto the ground. And then we had to scrape its body of hair, and images of the Crucifixion kept jumping into my brain—it was the only thing I knew that involved hanging up a body and doing these awful things to it. But this was normal, right? I mean, we ate bacon all the time. But then I knew Jewish people didn't eat pig and that Jesus started out as a Jew. I knew the pig was supposed to be the smartest animal in the barnyard. Why would they have these kids who are studying to be priests cutting open the smartest animal around? It really mixed me up, and not just for an hour or two. For days I had these images of the pig in my head, and nightmares too, all jumbled up with the Crucifixion. How in the world could something like this happen to a tough guy from Harlem, I wondered. So in a way this negative experience turned into a positive one because somewhere inside, I knew I was kinder than I let on. And I was okay with it. Years later— after I came through the darkness and was slowly brought back to life—I finally came to know a power greater than myself I call God. And then later—I mean *way* later—I remembered all these things. I accepted being more complex than I admitted to most people and that actually, maybe I could have been a priest, after all. And a good one, too. Except priests don't marry, and then I wouldn't have met my wife. And so I know it's all for the best. Even the darkness. It's all okay. Like they say at the end of a famous piece of AA literature: "We do not regret the past nor wish to shut the door on it." Because darkness told me about itself in ways I couldn't have known anything about it otherwise. And because eventually I'd be able to use this knowledge to help other human beings who were in places of darkness and wouldn't trust anyone who hadn't been there.

But back then I was just a kid from New York who got changed somehow by these experiences outside the city: seeing

Niagara Falls, getting this sense of forces in nature that could snap me like a twig; meeting other guys from other places, guys my own age who were struggling with joining the clergy instead of the "real" world; butchering that poor pig. All things I'd only have reason to think about way the hell up there at the edge of upstate New York back when I thought I wanted to be a priest

—∞∞∞—

By the time I got back to Queens I was fifteen or so and World War II was on. Suddenly it seemed like the world was holding its breath to see if we'd be speaking German the next day or not. Everybody was praying for our boys overseas. A blue star meant that a particular family had a son in the war, and a gold star meant that son was dead. Soon there was rationing and the streets got pretty quiet all of a sudden because most of the tough guys joined the army, or got drafted, or ran back to the old country, which was neutral. I was enrolled in Power Memorial High School, where my brother Jack was a Christian Brother and teaching a few courses. Not that this stopped me from my usual shenanigans, fighting and drinking whatever I could get my hands on—which wasn't much, or not enough, anyway. But since I was Brother Jack's kid brother, the other Brothers always wanted to take care of me, though they didn't take any nonsense. They had me kneeling on broomsticks and the like when I was caught cutting class. But I didn't give in. It was the stubbornness of that five-year-old kid who threw off his coat and wouldn't pick it up. Yelled at, spanked—didn't matter. I'd do it my way. Until my way had me dangling over an open grave. But I couldn't know anything about any of that yet.

I ended up getting a job at the A&P not too far from school. I cut classes all the time, and once in a while I had to duck when the Brothers came into the A&P. That was the only time I ever had to hide from having a job! True, the manager of the A&P used to get real annoyed when he'd see how much beer was being drunk downstairs. But it wasn't just me. I had a partner in crime. I forget his name now. He was the assistant manager, several years older than me, and a full-blown alcoholic, to boot. I didn't even know what an alcoholic was. In Irish culture "he drinks heavy" is about all you heard until it was "he died of the drink." Sure, the assistant manager drank heavy, so I figured if I drank with him there would be less for him to consume and I'd be doing him a favor. And if you believe that one, I'll tell you about the time I climbed Mount Everest! So he and I hit it off, and we'd wind up drinking a case of beer down in the basement maybe twice a week during the school year. That's when I started to slide by and get involved in a lot of other things, shooting craps and playing poker; but I managed to scrape through high school.

It sounds strange today, I realize, but the kind of trouble I was after at sixteen, seventeen, eighteen didn't much include women. Of course, once I was of age I'd go on double dates maybe with a buddy, take a couple of girls out for dinner. But the drinks came too slow for me. I'd excuse myself to wash my hands and have a couple of shots at the bar. Then more times than not I'd forget about the date and go up the street to a real drinking establishment, leave my friend holding the bag. And the bill! The upshot was, I travelled faster alone. And fast was how I liked it.

So finally I got that high school diploma and started to work with the Teamsters in Brooklyn at the terminal there, on Tenth Avenue. I was on the night shift, working for this candy company that made chewing gum, something like Chiclets. It got so I couldn't stand the sight or smell, let alone the taste. I was supposed to be at work at 11:30 p.m. or quarter to 12:00, but I would wind up getting down there maybe 1:00 in the morning. Pop was a big shot in the union, so the boss looked the other way. That is, until I pushed it too far. Soon I was in deep trouble with the higher-ups, and they started breathing down my old man's neck.

My folks had a candy store in Queens and I worked there for a while; but it seemed I was running more poker games and craps games in the back room than I was selling candy at the cash register. Then I was moonlighting as a bookie, taking bets for guys in the neighborhood; and when that got out the honeymoon with my father was over. I was back on Pop's bad side, and I stayed there, I regret to say, for a long, long time.

Trouble seemed to have it in for me. I kept getting in deeper and deeper. My blackouts became more frequent. I found myself sleeping on park benches, waking up not knowing what day it was, but knowing—the moment I opened my eyes—I was in trouble. Deep trouble. So I was running around, which was painful when I was hung over, trying to put out fires. I heard somewhere in some gin mill once that when a forest fire gets bad enough it actually travels underground. So you can have guys with trucks full of water hosing the perimeter like crazy, but the fire will actually sneak under all that and pop up in trees a couple of hundred feet away. Then those firefighters, they're surrounded. Well, that's what my life started to feel like. I'd try to take care of the trouble around my last bender, but there'd be too much of it—until its heat went underground and started breaking out in places I'd never been anywhere near. Not that I could remember, anyway. Of course, I'd have to have a drink or two just to face the day—and those tasted so good, I'd have to have another couple, and then another couple. And then I was off to the races. My drinking was out of control. It was like the horse was riding the rider. I was in debt with everybody, liked by few.

And then, while having a beer at some dive one morning, this light went off in my head—and I had it! A solution too good to be true! Of course, the problem with solutions too good to be true is nine times out of ten, they are. But I had to learn that the hard way.

Drinking that not-so-cold beer first thing that morning—chances are it was the second or third beer—I was fed up. So fed up that I told my new best pal, the bartender, "I know! I'll try the service. The war's over. I'll get my life back together, get some discipline. Sure, that's the ticket! Hey! Make this a boilermaker, would ya? And don't let me have anymore, this is my last ten and I got to go join up!" The bartender looked at me like I'd just told him the ocean was made of water. Anyway, he said the shot was on him. And he wished me luck.

The truth is I'd tried a similar stunt before when I signed up for the National Guard in Jamaica, Queens, after a horrendous drunk a year before. I wound up at a training camp in upstate New York cooking in the kitchen up there, and I damned near burned the whole camp down. Things got out of whack. Fire and flames were flying all over. Of course, I was half in the bag and wasn't watching what I was doing. Naturally, the CO took a dim view of that.

Then I was up on the side of a mountain one time. I used to sneak down the cliff to a gin mill. But a couple of guys followed me down, and one or two fell and got hurt, and I got blamed for that. It was one thing after another.

I was always in hot water and always trying to get out of a jam; but now I'd decided to go into the service for real, which is another story.

First, I walked into the Navy recruiting office in Queens. They took one look at me and said, "What the hell do you want?" So I said, "I'm here to join up. I thought you needed guys."

They said, "Yeah, well we don't need anybody like you. Come back when you sober up, but not here. Go to another recruiting office." I felt a little humiliated after that, so I went to my brother's place for a shower and a shave, borrowed a clean shirt, had a coffee and some toast. I told my sister-in-law I was going to clean up my act. Then I went over to the Army office, gave the finger to the Navy guys as I walked by. Then I tried the office of the Army Air Corp, as it was called at the time, before it became the Air Force. And lo and behold, they took me.

Two

We're in the Army Now

I USUALLY DON'T TALK about my time in the Army too much because it's where the shame stuff starts in like an artillery bombardment, like a nightmare; but sometimes it was a boring nightmare. Now, if you want to know how something can be boring *and* terrifying, you want to try being an alcoholic in the Army. It's like you're falling off a cliff but never quite hitting the rocks. The MPs are always there shaking you awake just before that.

One of the first things I remember after signing up is getting on a troop train in New York with a bunch of other recruits bound for Texas. The train made a stop on the way, and there was a delay of maybe four or five hours during which there really wasn't much supervision. I made the most of the situation, got off the train and bought a couple bottles of whiskey. Naturally, a couple of us recruits got loaded. But we got away with it, and I started to figure the whole thing with the Army is going be a piece of cake.

Finally, we got to Texas and I got off at San Antonio—half in the bag, as usual. I walked over to this big, tall, muscled-up sergeant and I said to him, "You know, I think I've changed my mind. I don't think I want to go through with this thing anymore." He looked down at me and said, "Hey, sonny boy, you belong to me now. You're in the Army, and you made a commitment up in New York, and you're part of us now!" So that was my introduction to the Army. Trouble is, I'd shown my cards early and they were on to me, this loudmouth from New York that had to be watched.

I went through three months of boot camp where I did a lot of things I wasn't really used to. For instance, I found out what discipline was all about. I also found out that when new recruits came in, they'd have to do guard duty in the barracks. When it came to be my turn, I'd confiscate the new guys' alcohol and other valuables, and then I'd turn around and sell them back. So I was wheeling and dealing from the word "go."

When I finished boot camp, I was sent to Chanute Field up in Illinois to attend weather school. Somebody told me that was a good deal, but it didn't last long—maybe a year and a half. I wasn't weatherman material, they said. I didn't know all the clouds because I didn't study because I was drunk most of the time. But while I was there I buddied up with a couple of guys from Long Island. We'd get together on weekends, go up to Chicago on weekend passes and panhandle—tell people we got rolled the night before and didn't have any money to get back to camp. We'd wind up with about ten or fifteen bucks in our pockets, enough to get drunk.

Once I woke up in a workhouse in Chicago and my shoes were gone. So I got hold of a couple of MPs and said I needed a pair of shoes to get back to camp. They took one look at me and said, "Hey, buddy, you better take off the rest of the uniform and stop impersonating a soldier. Otherwise, we'll have to lock you up."

That wasn't my only run-in with the MPs. There were plenty more. I went AWOL one particular weekend. I left Chicago and wound up back in New York. My father got wind of it and called the cops on me. The upshot is, I was "escorted" through Grand Central Station in cuffs and leg irons by two MPs, one on either side of me, taking me back to Chicago. I was shaking pretty bad for not having a drink. People were looking at me like I was some kind of a murderer or something. Every time

I passed a woman with her family, she'd grab her kids to keep them away from me. I guess I had a nasty look on my face to begin with and maybe I smelled. So that was one experience I wished I was blacked out for—but the MPs weren't in a very hospitable mood, if you get my drift.

I did a lot of bad things in the service, and I didn't feel much guilt or remorse. To tell you the truth, most of the time I didn't feel a whole lot of anything. I was too busy getting drunk. So on the whole, the Army finally got pretty fed up with me; most of the higher-ups didn't want anything to do with me. But at the same time there were always other officers who wanted to take credit for straightening me out. The upshot is, believe it or not, I would get promoted and moved around a lot. Once I wound up as a supply sergeant for a Nebraska outfit where they seemed to like me just fine. I was in charge of supplies, so naturally, I had the perfect opportunity to play my games and manipulate the system.

One time a bunch of us enlisted guys went out with our CO, who was a top sergeant. He was one of these guys who was always trying to straighten me out. Like he thought if he could just get in my head and tighten one loose screw—bingo!—I'd be fixed. Almost like I was his pet project or something. So he comes out drinking with me and the guys one night. I don't think they liked it much, but I figured he was good for a few free drinks. And the weird thing is I almost wanted him doing that research of his. It was almost like some secret part of me agreed with him—that if you could just get inside my brain and tighten one little screw, you could fix me. Not that I'd ever admit such a thing.

So sure enough we get a little high, and the sarge is wasted. I mean legless. He didn't usually drink with Irishmen, I guess. Not and keep up, anyway. Suddenly, I was babysitting *him*, not the other way around. And the other guys go off and get into their own trouble—they can see the sarge and me have some business to attend to. So he's staggering, and I've got an arm around him, and he's dragging me all over the street. I wasn't the one staggering. I want to get that straight. I wasn't even half in the bag yet. But this voice in my head is telling me, "You gotta get the sarge home. He's gonna fall down and hit his head, and if he dies, they'll lock *you* up." I don't know why that thought popped into my head, but it did. So I'm taking him back to the base, when out of the corner of my eye I see this camera in a parked car. And I see the button lock is up, so I plop my load against the hood and tell him, "Wait here, Sarge." Then I just nonchalantly open the car door, grab the camera, slam the door, and away we go until a few minutes later I drop him off at his door.

Next morning everything is back the way the Army likes it: officers in charge, enlisted men taking orders. Me? I had an eye-opener and a beer with my eggs. Meanwhile the sarge has a hurting headful of postcard pictures from the night before, without the whole movie stringing them together, if you get me. No eye-opener for him. I can hear him snarling at the guys as I come in. "Where's Cusack—you clowns?" And they're looking at each other like, "Knew we shouldn't have gone out drinkin' with the CO. Always trouble when you try to mix in with the higher-ups."

So in I waltz, and he takes one look at me says, "Speak of the devil! Get the hell in here!" and orders me into his office. He's standing in the door, sweating like a pig, and his face is about five different shades of green with a lot of red at the neck, like the cops are coming for him or something. But I know the guys are sizing me up, and I have my reputation to worry about, a reputation that's maybe in some trouble since I was socializing with the CO, and look what comes of that. But I've been here before. I know this tune from the top. So I take a comb out of my back pocket, and comb back my hair, and wink at the guys; then put my hat back on and follow the sarge into the office, where he proceeds to slam the door.

"What the hell, Cusack! Okay! I know I was drunk last night. Trying to go where you animals go! But I didn't black out like you figured. Not me. No, I got a crystal-clear memory of you stealing something from a parked car, Cusack." And then he loses it. "AND JUST WHAT IS THAT ABOUT, YOU THUG?" So now he's in my face screaming bloody murder. "YOU REALIZE YOU WAS IN THE COMPANY OF YOUR COMMANDING OFFICER, AND IF YOU'D BEEN CAUGHT IT WOULD HAVE BEEN MY ASS ON THE LINE!"

Now this look comes over his face like he sees a ghost. His eyes are bulged open big as triple-A eggs. Suddenly he grabs onto my shoulders like a long-lost brother, and then he just sort of buckles at the knees, and his eyes roll back in his head. I grab him by the uniform and start yelling for help from the guys, who—of course—are listening at the door. They come bolting in just as the sarge loses consciousness. So here I am holding this dead weight, yelling for somebody to call an ambulance. But the guys are all standing there like statues, staring at me like I was Jesus stepped out of the tomb. So I lay the sarge on a desk and call for an ambulance. And from that point on I'm considered a hero. The guys think, whatever the hell I did, apparently it had something to do with the seizure, and that's reason enough for the rest of the company to buy me drinks for the rest of the month.

But the whole thing threw me for a loop. I didn't want to think about it, so I threw back those free drinks like water. I knew the sarge might die and that he'd only gotten into this mess because he wanted to straighten me out. But instead of helping, he ends up in the hospital! And instead of the MPs showing up and throwing me in the clink, I'm tossing back free drinks like they're going out of style. And the thing that really gets me nuts is remembering I had a feeling the sarge was going down. That's why I escorted him home. And here I am the cause of him going down—and it's almost like I saw it—like a blind seer sees into the future. So I found an ocean of alcohol and I waded into the ocean with my mouth wide open. In fact, the sarge pulled through. So my luck held again. And then I was offered another chance to move and hope the change would do me some good. In the rooms, we call this a "geographic cure" or "taking a geographic," moving somewhere new to get a fresh start and leave trouble behind. But if substance abuse is calling the shots, there's no real change and history repeats itself. So a "geographic cure" is usually no cure at all; it just slows down the inevitable. But by this time I wasn't even fooling myself anymore. Oh, I knew a change of address would be a good thing, all right, so this Molotov cocktail called Jim Cusack could go somewhere they'd never heard of him before.

⌾

Offered a chance to go overseas, I jumped. But before I left, my brother called me up to have a cup of coffee. Now, he already knows I'm not talking to the folks. I don't want any part of them and they don't want any part of me. But before I leave for France, my brother picked me up. As I got in the car I said, "Where are we going?" He said, "Out to see Mom and Pop. You have to do that before you leave." I said, "Well, I don't want to do that." And he said, "Tough. I'm you're older brother, and I say we go out for a visit. For all we know they'll have another war, and you'll get killed and Ma will blame me for her never seeing you again."

So we went out there, and it was kind of awkward. I stayed there for three or four days. I'd buy a bottle and drink it in plain sight. What? I was shipping out for Europe! I was a big deal! But actually, it was painful. Naturally, I had another bottle in my room—suitcase whiskey. The whole family was on edge, but I didn't care. I was getting out. Next thing you know I'd be overseas, and something good has to come of that—right? Something for the better? So there I went on my merry way, keeping up with my medicine and keeping those jitters a good couple of stiff drinks away.

No surprise, I was in trouble long before I get to France. I put together a craps game onboard the ship and cleaned out everybody throwing a couple of dice—total game of chance. Spooky stuff. I didn't need to collect a paycheck for the next month!

Once I got to France I was assigned to a communications unit. I did a lot of things there I'm not too proud of. I sold stolen Army goods on the black market. I ran a lot of craps games and poker games. I managed the supply house and had slush funds for all kinds of people. And I took a taste of all that, you can be sure.

One time I got so drunk, I crawled back to the barracks on my belly like a crocodile crawling up out of the swamp. They rushed me to the hospital and when I woke up there were all these doctors and nurses hovering over me, poking and prodding me, asking me questions like I was some kind of a freak. Finally, I got some nurse to level with me. She told me my alcohol blood level broke the record—the highest anyone ever heard of, and that I should be dead. Then sure enough the big cheese came in for a visit with a couple of doctors, and they told me I was a "statistical impossibility" and that I should be in the morgue. Like they're trying to find some fear or shame in me. But instead of being upset, I was thinking I was some kind of hero. They checked me out for the longest time, but I got back on my feet and—before you know it—I was out drinking again.

One time I was supposed to go up with a couple of other guys on a mission outside Paris. I wound up not going because our CO called the noncommissioned officers' club where we were drinking to tell me I was needed on the ground for a freight inspection the next morning. Ordinarily, I would have ignored the order, but for some reason I followed it and stayed on the ground. The flight that I would have taken with those guys exploded shortly after takeoff and everybody on board was killed. I had to get their names, these guys I'd been hell-raising with the night before, so their families could be contacted. I couldn't understand why I was saved. And maybe, just maybe a part of me was disappointed not to go out with my buddies like that, in a split second. No warning. No long good-byes. Without, that is, me having to burn in hell for doing the job myself. I was sort of on the edge of that thought when I went into a blackout or ten.

Another time I dodged the Reaper, I was home on leave and took my mother to see *How Green Was My Valley* for Mother's Day. I think it was the only time I ever did anything like that with my mother. And I remember realizing that as I kissed her good-bye. It was a Saturday night and I was supposed to meet some buddies at a bar. When I arrived I learned they'd been involved in a car accident. One of them was killed and the other two were maimed. What was this about? I needed the answer! But my drinking was so bad, I didn't talk to the priests anymore. Or if I went it, was BS I was confessing to—nothing with an open heart. My insides were blocked off. The only way in there was to get blotto, but then I'd go into a blackout, so any temporary state of honesty with myself would be wiped out once the curtain came down.

Today, when I look back at these incidents, I realize maybe God had a plan for me. I wasn't sure what was happening. I knew I was drinking heavily. I knew it was having an impact and I wasn't thinking straight. But I always figured I'd get around to straightening out soon, sometime after I found the next drink. I was a full-blown alcoholic, but I didn't realize it. I know that's hard to believe, but you have to understand that after the war, the free world was on a party. Sometimes even people who weren't alcoholics were drinking like alcoholics, so the real alcoholics weren't all alone in the bar yet. We hadn't been left holding the bag.

Other times, I found crazy situations which seemed to justify my crazy drinking. The Communists were very active in France at the time. I used to get plowed at the bar while talking to myself in the mirrors—working myself into these rages. The bartenders were French, so I had some trouble getting them riled up. Then I'd march into the middle of these rallies and break them up. I'm lucky I wasn't killed. I'd just go berserk—start taking guys down left and right like the old days when I had a brick for a fist. The French guys were small and not too tough. Napoleon, they say, had all the big guys in France killed, marching them out in the first wave. All except Charles de Gaulle's great-grandfather, right? So I'd be knee-high in these punched-out little Communists, that is, before the mob got too big or the MPs showed up with their handcuffs.

There was a file a mile long on me these COs would take out and bang their fists on while raking me over the coals. They'd sneer at me with disgust and tell me I was a disgrace to the uniform, that the Communist issue was under careful study. And who did I think I was, anyway? General Patton or something? Who did I think I was, judge and jury, when I didn't even understand French? Meanwhile, I was messing with a sacred memory! The sacrifice of thousands of dead American heroes! And what did I have to say for myself?

You'd think the BS explanations would stick in my throat by now, but no—up they'd come, shiny and new. Thing is, I think I believed them half the time. I remember writing letters a couple of times, apologizing to the CO. I think they were ignored mostly. You know, "Add it to the file." Maybe they just thought I was some kind of wacko, which no doubt, I was. But honestly, I really didn't think I was doing that much wrong. I thought I was serving justice, doing my time. The truth is, I couldn't wait to get out of the service. By now my father had received letters from my COs saying what a disgrace I was to the armed forces, and could he do anything about it? He was totally in the dark and didn't know how to respond.

I'd signed up for four years. Then Korea came along, and my tour was extended another year, so I spent a total of five years in the service from the age of eighteen to twenty-three. My claim to fame was that I managed to get out of the service with an honorable discharge as a staff sergeant!

Finally, I was discharged at Fort Dix, New Jersey, and some corporal was looking at my record and at how many times I'd been in the guardhouse. So he starts to give me a hard time. He's a corporal and I'm a sergeant, but I end up chewing the guy out. Truthfully? I really wanted to beat the bejesus out of the guy. Because he was trying to make me feel small, and I guess I'd had a few drinks. Anyway, this colonel overhears me letting loose on a corporal with both barrels. So he pulls me aside and looks at me really sternly and I think, "Uh-oh, here we go again. Me and my big mouth." Then he sticks out his hand and says how proud he is to meet me and he says, "We need more men like you." And he goes on to tell me that if I reenlist, he'll put me in charge of his outfit. So I laugh and shake his hand, and thank him just the same. I tell him no, I'd had my fill of the Air Force. Then he salutes me and I salute him. It was nuts! I'm completely out of order, and here some cowboy of a colonel wants to take a wacko like me and put him in charge of an entire outfit. It's stuff like this that really screws a guy up. In fact, it can feed your ego and confusion and keep you out there drinking longer. And I'm sorry to say it, but the service was full of this kind of stuff.

When I got home I went back to Harlem and found a few uncles who hadn't drunk themselves to death yet. I was in uniform and we did some "old-fashioned celebrating" with the usual results. These guys had been my heroes, but they were dropping like flies. When I was a kid, I was helping out one uncle in a garage once, and he fell down and had a seizure. In fact, he wouldn't live out the month. But he falls hard on the cement, so I rush and kneel beside him and he says, "Jimmy, get me a drink, lad! Get me a whiskey!" So I get a bottle from somewhere and I pour him a drink. There he is lying on the greasy floor, near death. And he throws back the drink and let's out this contented sigh, like, "Okay. I'm ready." Tell you the truth, I was in awe of him. I thought, "This is how it's done. This is how a tough guy lives and dies."

Of course, the minute I hit New York my brother and his wife were worried about me, and my folks weren't too happy either. After a few days I took a furnished room in Queens, and it was pretty much downhill from there. Along the way I met my first wife. Her folks had a place right next to a bar I frequented, and I guess I wasn't too loaded when I met her. Pat was this beautiful girl, maybe a couple of years younger than me. She was living with her parents and she wanted out. She didn't have the money to do it on her own. I guess maybe I presented myself okay on the outside, better than how I felt on the inside, that is. Here

I was, fresh out of the service, on a party . . . Why not? I guess maybe the nutcase who went berserk when drunk was taking a little rest. Honestly, I wasn't too sure what Pat saw in me, but what tough guy ever admits to something like that? All I know is, she wanted to get married.

It wasn't until years later I found out this lovely young woman had tragically been raped by a group of men when she was very young. The perpetrators went back to another country so there was nobody for me to go kill. But I wouldn't know about this tragedy, really, until it was too late. So there we were. Me, a crazy alcoholic who didn't know what the word meant. And her, a lonely, scared, and deeply scarred young beauty with a ton of intimacy issues. The truth is, it wasn't much of a marriage. I was damaged goods myself—though I wouldn't admit it to anybody. Certainly not to a woman. Especially if she's my wife. Long story short, we were together only a little more than a year. It was like we only had three or four conversations we knew, and most of them ended up with me crazy drunk, smashing things, and her running out the door with a raincoat thrown on over her dressing gown, running back to her folks' place where I found her. So before long we broke up. Seemed like for good. And then I really went to hell with myself.

Soon I was drinking around the clock, just going crazier and crazier. I'd find myself sitting alone in the apartment with a club in one hand and a bottle in the other, waiting for the radiator to hiss. When it does I say aloud, "When that little guy comes out from behind that radiator, I'm gonna clobber him good!" Alcohol had me in a stranglehold. It didn't do what it used to do. When the bottle was on the high side, I was okay, but when it was on the low side, I knew I'd have to go out and get more. I didn't know what was happening to me. I was nuts. I was on the edge of throwing in the towel.

I wish I could say to you I know exactly what happened when, but that would be a lie. For a while my life got to be like a blender drink. Not that I ever drank that stuff, unless someone else was buying. That's right, a blender drink—lots of alcohol and sugar and sour mix and ice and whatever else was lying around. Sure, I got sent away a couple of times. I came back. I was drinking again. I got dry on another visit to some other summer camp for alcoholics. I was working, then I was out of work. Yeah, I got married. Then I was single again. It was always like, where am I this time? And why am I alive still? How much does it take for a guy to get dead anyway? And why can't I seem to drink enough to do the trick?

One thing I missed from the service was the camaraderie. I'd lost touch with my old drinking buddies and I hadn't gone out of my way to make new ones. Tell you the truth, I wasn't very likable and I didn't bother trying to be. As far as jobs were concerned, the bosses were skeptical. As a union head my father had influence, but a lot of guys were inclined to judge me based on "past performance." Now, even though I'd been a troublemaker in the service, there was this begrudging fondness for me there—like I was one guy you could always tell some whacko story about. But that stuff didn't fly in the civilian world. I had to bite the bullet and admit nobody was buying my BS anymore. And the worst part about it? Those lousy opinions people had about me? Well, for the most part, I agreed with them.

The drinking was constant. But I wasn't walking around bombed all the time; instead, I was "mochus"—couldn't get drunk and couldn't get sober. Alcohol didn't do the trick for me anymore, but I had no choice. I had to drink. Take my word— you don't want to see what happens to a guy who drinks like me and stops cold. I'd had the DTs a few times already when I was locked up by the MPs. Enough to know I didn't want any repeats of that particular experience.

The first time I got locked up again stateside, I wound up at the local precinct near Kings County Hospital in Queens, New York. I recognized a couple of cops there who didn't like me too well. One of them was a guy I knew from high school, and he "suggested" I go to Kings County to get some help—so that was my introduction to detox. There were two stabbings while I was there, a couple of brawls. One guy was stomped into unconsciousness. Another guy was in there with me and we walked around back to back, like a set of Siamese twins, this being the only way to be sure we didn't get jumped. He was a vicious guy, I soon found out—meaner than a junkyard dog—and that was just fine with me. That SOB was watching my back, so the meaner the better. With both of us going through the DTs, mind you. I remember thinking we were a gigantic crab, him and me. Each in control of a pincer. It was Nutsville in there, all right. And I kept seeing the face of this cop who didn't like me, and the sweet little smile that came over his face when he said: "I think what this guy needs is a little visit to Kings County." I wanted to get out and go strangle that guy. But in the meantime, I needed to sweat out the DTs and stay alive. To do that I needed my junkyard dog chained to my back. We'd have these long conversations with our eyes on guard. He told me every time he got drunk, he would pick up a gun and he would put it in his wife's mouth and threaten to blow her head off to scare the hell out of her. And I said, "What a bitch you married! Imagine her putting you in a place like this just for doing something like that!" I knew I was talking crazy talk, but you need backup in a place like that. So you sympathize with a lunatic if you need to, to keep his loyalty.

When they released me, they told me I could have a beer every now and then, and I would be okay. There wouldn't be any problem. Maybe now you realize the total lack of any understanding—even by the so-called "experts"—of what alcoholism is.

After my experiences at Kings County I didn't have any desire to do anything about my drinking. The rest of the world just didn't get it. I needed this stuff—and I mean I needed a good supply of it to get me through the day, and an even better supply to get me passed out for a few hours at night. For an alcoholic, that's not a drinking problem. Getting sober is the problem, and you can only avoid that by drinking around the clock. I realized that I was a little different from other people in this regard, but this was just the reality of the situation.

Of course, when I get back to my father's house I immediately go back to my usual tricks. He gets fed up, and soon I have my second experience with AA. Maybe Pop knew a guy in the Teamsters who was in the program. None of it's too clear. Anyway, a husband and wife take me out to a place called Charlie Smith's in Northport, Long Island. On the drive out the guy turns to me and says, "Jim, you don't know how much you're helping me." So I look at him like he's got two heads, and then I figure out maybe Pop paid him off to have me stashed. It would be years before I could wrap my head around the notion that somebody helping somebody else might actually help the helper. So I went to Charlie Smith's and stayed a week. The DTs paid another visit, and soon I was walking a dog that didn't exist that I named Snake Eyes. Snake Eyes would bite you bad if you didn't do what his master said, and his master was me. Charlie Smith's was kind of like a park. I looked around at all the people, and I thought it was a good thing they were here. I figured a good drink would kill most of them. So I was like this walking, talking combination of lunatic and wiseguy. When I got out, a cousin of mine said he'd take me in at his place. I lasted there for about two weeks until he told me I had to leave because I had gotten into his liquor cabinet. The agreement was I could stay as long as I wanted as long as I didn't have anything to drink. I think my wife took me back for a minute, then she left again.

Not too soon after that I lost the will to live. I would go to sleep, hoping—actually praying to God, to please just let me go to sleep and never wake up. You hear a lot about this "prayer for death" in later phases of alcoholism, from those of us who survive, that is. There are those who never make it, who had that prayer answered.

This is around the time my story gets pretty mixed up. But that's what life had become—a bad joke looking for a punch line I could never find. But finally, there I was alone in this apartment, sitting in a chair, staring at the radiator waiting for the little guy to crawl out from behind it. Knowing the bottle was going to be empty in another minute. Wondering how I'm going to get money to buy a new one or if I should just kill myself and leap into hell feet first. That was my defining moment. The bottom of that bottle.

THREE

First Light

MAYBE I WAS DESPERATE enough finally to reach out. Did I have a home? No, I didn't have a home anymore. Not so long before, I'd had one—an apartment, or was that another time? Right, I'd had a place not so long ago. I lived there with a stranger called my wife. But she'd finally had enough and left, went back to her mother's. So I hit the streets, gradually. Stopped paying rent, and then I was *on* the streets. I was panhandling. I slept on benches in these little parks in Queens, not far from where my folks lived. I couldn't stay with them anymore; my father wouldn't have it. I slept in unlocked cars, in doorways, in flophouses. I was floating around just looking for my next drink—wine mostly, because I could stay drunk for a couple of days on wine. If I got enough in my system, even drinking water would knock me for a loop. With whiskey, I'd wake up poisoned, and I'd have to start over, chasing the buzz. And it's expensive. With wine, I stayed drunk for forty-eight hours on two, maybe three rotgut bottles.

The truth is, yes, I really just wanted to die. This was a death wish all right, and I'd had it for a while. At first it had a mask on called "my next drink," but the mask finally came off and Death was sitting there with me. I didn't mind—I knew the score. Sure, this is the way my uncles went, how tough guys went—the Irish way, and all they'd say of me was, "he died of the drink."

After the discipline of the Army I got swallowed up by the street. I tried a little while. Did this and that. And then I just gave up on myself and everything else. Until finally one day, instead of begging the money to buy a bottle and watch the radiator, I called up my sister-in-law. Sure, I was desperate and this was the one person who never gave up on me completely. No one else wanted me. My family had had it, and I understood that right down the line. I'd had it with me, too. But this one day, some survival instinct pushed me to call up Elaine, and she encouraged me as best she could, told me, "I'm going to have to clear this with your brother but . . . It'll be okay. I'll make sure. But you're not going to be able to drink here, Jimmy." She was always of a mind to give me another chance. To this day, I don't know exactly why. I guess she figured she could sober me up enough to get me on my feet, get me back to work.

So I went to my brother's place and went four or five days without taking a drop. Of course, I knew what I was in for—the tremors, the dry mouth, the shakes, the itches, the sweats, the fears, and then of course, the main attraction: you go nuts, start seeing things that aren't there. I greeted a delivery boy at my brother's front door with a knife in my hand when my sister-in-law told me calmly, "Put the knife down, Jimmy. There's nobody there."

That puts me in mind of trips I made over the Hudson River, I can't even remember when. Over there I got sober at meetings in a home for the criminally insane, complete—you bet—with the DTs. I talked to some of the guys who were there because of their dangerous behavior under the influence, nothing I knew anything about, right? They were labeled "criminally insane," but some of them truly wanted help. I recognized their drinking patterns were a lot like mine. Still, they had the guts to walk into an AA meeting looking for an answer. Any AA meeting I'd ever been in, I had laughed at. But maybe the joke was on me. Then, I met with a whole different group who had absolutely no recollection of the crimes they'd committed. They had no memory of any wrongdoing, motive, or intent.

But these meetings, hopeless as they seemed for most of these guys, cleared something up for me. I felt like I belonged in the first group, or I was closer to them, anyway, than the second. I knew I had a problem, one that maybe, just possibly could be addressed. I remember what a huge relief it was when I realized I wasn't nuts—I was sick.

So there I was with my brother, Jack, and my sister-in-law, Elaine, sweating out the devil, but knowing I was safer with them than anywhere else. If I didn't drink, they wouldn't call the MPs or the cops. If I didn't drink, they wouldn't send me away. I was with family. They knew I was sick, not crazy. Was it my sister-in-law's threat of kicking me out if I drank which forced me to put the bottle down for good? Or had I finally just had enough? Finally ready to go through withdrawal and come out the other side, get that hellhound off my tail once and for all! Was I ready this time—for real? Maybe I was.

Sure enough, staying with my brother's family, I started to come around. They had a new son, this beautiful little baby boy—my nephew, Kevin, whose wedding we attended forever ago. In fact, we were just visiting with him last weekend—he's sixty now with grandchildren of his own. Back then in my dark times Elaine trusted me to hold him. But I have to admit I didn't feel too good about that. It made me nervous. No one else would let me near him, but she trusted me to hold him, and well, holding a baby is a profound experience. You feel this tiny, precious being in your arms, this goo-goo, gah-gah thing filled with happiness that brings hope into every corner of this awful world. But it was like she wanted to force me to feel a piece of that hope without saying a word about it, for me to know that she trusted me with her infant son—the most precious thing in her life. It cemented this bond between us. She and I had our own rapport and she never gave up on me. She was like the sister I never had. It's true, I felt unworthy to touch anything so perfect and fragile as that baby, but she wouldn't let me go there. She'd just stick him in my arms, and there he was, like it or not. It meant a lot. Like a ray of sunlight at the bottom of a black pit. How did it get there, where did it come from? There's only one place it *could* come from. From above. The first time I even started to think maybe I might have a chance was this period, when I was holding this nephew of mine.

My self-esteem was in the toilet and I needed to fix that, right? So—foolishly—I thought I could go back to work. Bring in a few dollars to put on the table. My brother and Elaine lived right on the border of Long Island and Queens. When I left their house to go find work in the city, I was trembling so badly I couldn't hold a cup of coffee without spilling it all over the train platform. I didn't want a drink, but I needed one. I took the train to the bus and got off at Roosevelt Avenue near where my folks lived. Later on I'd hear about our disease pushing you into dangerous places and setting you up for the kill. That day my disease had me in the crosshairs, all right. Suddenly, I felt like I absolutely had to have a drink. Just throw one back, I said to myself. Buy a pack of gum, lighten the load, and be back out and on my way. Just one—but I knew that was malarkey.

On the corner was a gin mill, Cusack & Dowling's, the place where I once convinced the owner we were long-lost cousins and he bought me a few rounds. Today, I didn't have money except for the train, but this plan takes shape anyway, the old wiseguy who can always find a way. Then this other voice says, "But you can't drink, what're you talking about?" But the old voice talks over it: "Sure. I hand him the old line about him and me being long-lost relatives, the Cusacks from County Clare." And seeing the barroom there, knowing it was cool and dark inside with those Budweiser neon lights all red in the windows, maybe even the smell of the place, it's working me, all right, working me good. I try fighting back. Because I don't want a drink, I just have to have one. I just have to. And sure enough, my feet are taking me closer towards the place, and I'm sweating now. Struggling. I want to run the other way, but I can't pass by this joint without going in. And if I go in—it's over. I know that. But I can't stop my feet. So they're going in, which means I'm going down. I can't stop myself. I got my hand on the door and I'm about to pull it open when for some reason I think of this priest, Father Parks. Then out of the corner of my eye I see a pay phone at the corner and I let go of the gin mill's door and push past it. Inside the phone booth there's a huge phone book chained to the counter. I look up the parish number, drop a dime in the slot, make the call, and sure enough, Father Parks picks up the phone. He asks me how I am and then where I am, so I tell him. He says, "Go to your father's house and I'll have somebody meet you. Go there right now, Jimmy." So I call up my mother and tell her I just spoke to Father Parks and he's sending somebody over to help me with my drinking. It's the first time I ever just say it out loud to my mother—that I'm in trouble with the drink. Somehow that simple statement was a breakthrough. And she gets it, my mother's no dummy. So she says, "Of course, Jimmy. Come on over. Come over right now!" I can hear my father in the background say, "He ain't stayin' here." So I tell my mother I get the deal, I'll come over but I won't stay. So I go over to my folks' place, and the "somebody" who shows up to take me to a meeting comes in, and without saying a word he looks me in the eye and puts out his hand, so I take it and we shake.

Maybe you'll know what I mean when I say there are a lot of different ways to shake hands with a guy. First of all, back then most people took one look at me and got as far away from me as they could. Why? Because it was pretty easy to see that I was trouble and nothing but. I was mean, angry, and scared—and that made me angrier still. Yet this guy Joe just walks up to me like he was walking up to a wounded, snarling dog, but he won't buy the snarl—he won't even buy the wound. It was like he knew something I didn't know. There was this calm assurance about him. He put out his hand, and I knew he was willing to take a chance on me. So I took his hand. And it's a solid handshake. Not like he's showing off. You know, not trying to grind my knuckles to powder, but manly. Solid. Honest. Later on I found out Joe was one of the very first to get sober through the steps of Alcoholics Anonymous. Turns out he was some kind of legend, but you'd never know it. He certainly never put that out. All I know is that he asked me to tell him a little about myself and the trouble I was in. So I did, and then after a while he said we should go to a meeting and he's going to be my sponsor. Not that I knew what that meant. Today I know I owe him my life and will be forever grateful to his memory, though back then I didn't know what gratitude meant, either. I'd been looking for somebody who'd do me the favor of taking away my life, not giving it back. But I was so mochus, I didn't know if I was coming or going. I take that back. When Joe walked through the door I knew one thing was certain: we were going to a meeting that night, and it was going to be different from the meetings I'd been to before.

And that's how my sober journey began.

I really knew nothing about the program and less about myself. In the rooms they say that once you start drinking (or using) on a daily basis, you stop maturing. I didn't believe this at first, but over the years I have found it to be true. Now, I started drinking on a daily basis at about twelve—so emotionally, that's the age I was when I took my last drink. And when you think about it—when you see me sitting there waiting for that little guy to come out from behind that radiator, it sort of makes sense. I'm a big, drunk, delusional bully of about twelve! So waking up to a grown-up world as a grown-up guy without a bottle in my hand—was a struggle, to say the least. But I just kept following this guy Joe to meetings.

That very first night he came over to my folks' I told him some of the rotten things I'd done that I was not too proud of. So I got some of that heavy stuff off my chest. I didn't get everything out, not by a long shot. But I told him about people I'd hurt. Women I'd abused. Things I had stolen—I mean, I was never a second-story man—never broke and entered, at least not to steal; but if stuff was lying around, it found its way into my pocket pretty quick. And Joe just took all this stuff in, didn't say much, just listened. So I heaped quite a load on him—I mean, I didn't hit him with the deep, dark stuff—though eventually I did. But I let him know what a conniver I was, and it didn't seem to phase him. Though he admitted to me later that if he knew at the start what I eventually told him I'd done, he wouldn't have taken me on, wouldn't have had anything to do with me. Why? Because I was a vicious son of a bitch in a lot of ways. Especially in a blackout. And my blackouts might be two days, might be two weeks. There was no way of knowing.

There were times I'd report to work on jobs I'd been fired from. The head guy would look up at me and say, "What're you doing here?" And I'd say, "I'm here to work." And he'd say, "Who hired your sorry ass back to work? Not me. Get out of here and don't come back." People would tell me stuff I'd done in a blackout and I wouldn't believe it. Then someone else would tell me the same thing and I'd have to deal with the fact it was true. I was told I had run across Union Avenue as the cabs were screaming up to make the green light, hoping some taxi would run me down and kill me. One night a cabbie screeched to a halt and screamed at me. I pulled him out from behind the wheel and beat him senseless. Another time I came to in the police station just as the sarge was almost singing it, "You really did it this time, Cusack!"

"Did what?"

"We don't know if that guy you hung up on the fence is going to live or die!"

"What guy on what fence?"

"Jesus Christ," the sergeant muttered under his breath. "Lock him up and call his father, for all the good it'll do."

Looking back, I think maybe I was split into two different people the instant I saw this guy Joe. A part of me knew he had something that could help me. And a part of me didn't believe anything could help—and that even if there was such a thing, I didn't deserve it. And yes, the dark part almost completely outweighed the light. So it was the dark me that was daring this guy Joe to walk away. So I could prove that all this Twelve-Step brotherly love was a crock. And like I said, there was a part of Joe that was disgusted, all right. I wasn't even twenty-four years old, and the stuff I told him gave him nightmares, I'd bet. But the strange part of it is that our relationship grew. And we could feel it. The more crap I piled on his head, the more poison he knew I was spilling from my guts, and in my own way, the more courage I was pulling up from somewhere to get this poison out. So he ended up having this weird admiration for that courage, same as I had my own weird admiration for the fact that he could take all this junk in and not fold his hand and ask for a new deck. The result being, this bond of trust developed between us. Maybe I wouldn't have used the word "trust" back then, but that's what it was. At first it felt darker than trust. Because I still had to contend with this tough guy in me, the guy who knew he was doomed and didn't want to be teased with salvation because it wasn't in the cards. How could it be, with what I'd done? So the dark part was pushing Joe to give up on me. I could feel myself doing just that, sometimes. Like a voice said, "Oh, you can handle that, huh? Okay, how about this? Now tell me I'm really an okay guy. Go ahead. Tell me I'm 'sick as my secrets.' Tell me God loves me no matter how far down the ladder I've gone. Even after this one, huh, Joe? God loves me still, even after I did this?"

Because I knew in my gut God had given up on me, just as I'd given up on Him. Not that I stopped believing in Him. I still believed, somewhere deep down in the sewer of my soul. Even down there, even in my darkest hour, I still believed. But I knew I was on God's blacklist, and when I took the trouble to think about it I remembered why, and that's when I felt I didn't deserve to get sober. I wasn't sure where I was or where I wanted to be. I think, really, I still wanted to die. Because—as must be pretty obvious by now—I didn't like me. Not one bit. So why should anyone else like me? Maybe this guy Joe was like the guys on Division Street in Chicago who'd give me a bottle in exchange for me pretending I was dead already while they did to me whatever they liked, so long as the bottles kept coming. It hardly mattered because what they did, they did to a dead man. A dead man still breathing, that is. But that's just the malarkey the alcohol told me. Because I wasn't dead. I was alive. And I carried the shame of it all. And the silence and self-hatred hovering around the shame until finally I spilled my guts about that to Joe and to other alcoholics, who I eventually learned did what I'd done to get a bottle—which is, whatever you have to do to get a bottle. Hating ourselves a little more. "One day at a time." What a bunch of malarkey it all was, this Twelve-Step junk! And yet it was all I had. Sometimes I felt like a total chump going to these meetings at all. But slowly—and I mean really slowly—I started to come around, and once in a while it seemed like I could see a little light at the end of the tunnel.

But the really weird part is that by the time Joe finally admitted, if he'd any idea of what I'd done with my life, he'd never have taken me on—by then we were laughing about it over coffee after a meeting. And we could see it was sort of like a test or a trick God played on us both that neither one of us had any control over, but that it all happened for a reason. My hand on the door of the gin mill. The face of Father Parks coming into my brain. My letting go of the door to the barroom and walking to the corner and picking up the pay phone. Father Parks calling up Joe and saying, "I got a tough nut for you, Joseph . . . you game? " And sure, by then I trusted the guy. Though maybe I wouldn't yet say the word out loud.

Fact is, I knew if I picked up a drink, I was finished. So there was no going back for me one way or the other. I just kept on going to meetings, and that self-hatred with its death wish for a chaser, it slowly started to lighten up. It didn't go away, mind you. But I didn't feel like I was in total blackness anymore. It was like the room was still dark but the curtains were streaked with gray, so dawn couldn't be too far off. Soon the birds in the park would go nuts chirping and singing all at once and you'd know the long night was almost over. And you'd see some light in the window. A little bit of light—just as you finally fall off to sleep. And it's real sleep, not passing out. Real, honest-to-God sleep. A real night's sleep . . . talk about a gift!

It's around this time I began to loosen up a little bit and start to get some hope, when I first thought to myself, "Maybe I can get this." There were no guarantees. I didn't know how I was going to get it. I didn't know what I was going to do with myself if I *did* get it. Take, for example, my first dry Christmas. I came into the rooms in October, and that first holiday season I was really upside-down. I was staying at my mother and father's house, and I felt like a bump on a log. I was fidgety—didn't know what to do or say or what not to do or say. I couldn't figure out if I even belonged there or whether it wouldn't just be better to end it all, for everybody's sake. But then I'd burn in hell for sure. Like I wasn't in hell already?

It was slow going for me to forgive myself, that's the bottom line. Sure, I could say, "This is a disease," but when I looked back at what I did, I just buried my head. I can't tell you if I prayed much about it. I didn't know where to go with it all except to the only place I *could* go which was to a meeting, then to the coffee shop sober guys hung around. Meetings were scarce in those days and anonymity was fiercely protected. AA was a huge experiment; no one had ever before freely admitted to being an alcoholic, like guys in jail never admit to being guilty. The whole thing was risky; but pretty quickly, the rewards outweighed the risks. Then it got to be a routine: go to a meeting, then have coffee with Joe, maybe with some other guys in the program. But sometimes I still felt like a faker.

I knew when I woke up in the morning I'd still be the guy who'd done all this stuff. I couldn't turn that around or change any of that, so what could I do? For a long time there wasn't any answer except like they said, "Meeting makers make it" and "Keep coming back." So I did. But I was still skeptical. I still thought, "These guys are all bullshit." This "grateful alcoholic" crap made me want to puke. I didn't want to hear it. But then gradually, I started to get a sober history. And the program slogans almost stopped rubbing me the wrong way most of the time. I realized maybe these guys were a little further along than me. Either that or they were zombies, like from *Invasion of the Body Snatchers*. But I knew I'd been a miserable zombie running across Union Avenue in a blackout, trying to get a cab to run me down and kill me. Given a choice, I thought, I'd rather be a happy zombie—like one of these goddamned grateful alcoholics.

FOUR

The Road to Recovery

THE FIRST FIVE YEARS of recovery sucked. I kept going anyway. I was squirrely; I'd jump at the least noise. I remember wanting to get out for a walk but not feeling safe with alcohol for sale and all the ads for it everywhere. So I paced instead. Sometimes I went up and down the stairs just to wear myself out. The bottom line is, I remember fighting a drink on a daily basis for the better part of five years.

My parents saw my struggle. And probably heard about it too from my brother, Jack, and Elaine, the sister I never had. I knew my mother, for one, had all her friends at church praying themselves silly to keep me sober. My father was rooting for me too, no doubt. But in a quieter way. I kind of felt like he might've had a side bet going with God, in case I didn't make it. You know, he didn't want to put every last dollar on the underdog—which is what I was—even if the underdog happened to be his son. Why? Because he was a realist. A praying man, yes, but he also knew he might have to be the strong one if I didn't pull through. In that case he'd need to be the rock for my mother. Maybe he could get her through it, maybe not. Some mothers survive such a tragedy while others just curl up and die inside and wait for the Lord to take them. Dark stuff, I know. The thing is, just because you're not waking up with hangovers doesn't mean you don't go to the dark places anymore. You do. Except now you don't have your painkiller to numb you from the fear waiting in the dark place. And you can get stuck there. Believe me, getting sober is not all miracles and rainbows—and it isn't for the weak of heart.

I remember one time I called up my sponsor and told him this program of his was a crock, and he could shove it where the sun don't shine. I was all worked up, and I forget what else I said, but I let him have it. I was about to slam down the phone and go buy a bottle. But my sponsor, Joe L., was a "scientist of the soul." So he bounces off the ropes with this surprise punch—doesn't telegraph it, and I never saw it coming. Truth is, I never saw one before quite like it. And I never had the guts, not in sixty years of sobriety, to ever throw this punch myself. But as I say, this guy Joe was a master. It was like he had a horseshoe in his right glove and here it comes, straight for my jaw.

"You want a drink?" Joe yells at me through the phone, "Fine! I got a bottle right here. Come on over and get it. It's for company. So it ain't even been cracked because I don't see company no more. Too busy trying to put idiots like you back together. You want a drink, you quitter? It's a fifth of Four Roses. That good enough for you, chump? Better than the crap you were swilling, waiting for the guy behind the radiator, I'll bet. But that was then and this is now—right, Cusack? You're a changed man. Am I right? And no, the booze won't turn you back into any of that. Nah, drink won't take *you* down! Why should it? It wasn't like it took you down every time you had that first jolt. Hell no, it only took you down on Tuesdays and Thursdays, right, Jim? Every other day of the week you had a shot or two and then put the cork back in the jug and put it back on the shelf, isn't that right? Besides, you been sober for a few years now. So you're smarter and stronger than the booze now, aren't you, Jim? Sure you are! So here's the deal. I'll cut you loose and wish you luck. But you got to have the guts to look me in the eye before you take the first drink. Okay? So come on over here. But go get a hamburger first because I ain't feeding you. Get it? Then come on here and drink like a man. You hear me, Cusack?

Huh? What's wrong? Cat got your tongue? I'm telling you I got a bottle for you! Just come on and get it! Hey! I'm talking to you, Cusack? You there?"

So I said, "Yeah, I'm here." And I hung up the phone. Then it was like I was sleepwalking. I just did what Joe said. I went out and got a hamburger—didn't order a beer though they had it there. Then I followed my feet to the subway and got off at the stop for Joe's place. I walked up the three flights and knocked on the door, and I heard Joe say, "It's open."

So I walk in, and he's alone in the kitchen, though I could hear the TV behind another door. He's just sitting at the kitchen table smoking a cigarette, staring at me. And there it was on the table, the Four Roses, unopened, just like he said. "So you want it in a shot or a water glass, Jim? Or maybe you just want to take a long slug out of the bottle and just get back to business for real. Your call. I don't have all night, so let me know and let's get this over with. I got another sponsee who wants to go to a meeting."

I stand there looking at the bottle, then at Joe, then back to the bottle, and then back to Joe. It was like one of those dreams where you're stuck someplace. Your feet are glued to the floor in some kind of nightmare you can't wake up from.

"Cusack!" Joe yells finally. "You drunk already or what?"

"No," I said. "I did just like you told me."

He says, "Well, if you want it, here it is! But I got better things to do than hang around with a drunk like you, so crack the bottle and get started. Tell you what, you can take the whole damn thing. I don't want it here no more. TAKE THE DAMN THING—COME ON! You want a drink, well, here it is. WHAT'RE YOU WAITING FOR?"

So what do I do? This tough guy with a fist like a brick? This stubborn Mick I wake up inside of every day of this life? What do I do but break down and start to bawl like a baby. Now Joe stands up, steps around the table, and takes me in his arms. He closes this cast-iron embrace around my back and he says, "It's okay, you big galoot. It's okay."

I'm sobbing like I just lost my mother. So he loosens his grip but doesn't let go. He holds on like a fighter in a clinch, and now he says it quiet, like a boxer when no one, not even the referee can hear—he says, "I been there. We all have, Jim. Every last one of us. Now listen. Listen to what I tell you now. Okay?"

So I nod my head, yes. Sniffing like a snot-nosed kid as Joe, real quiet, says it right in my ear. He says, "The devil don't come for small fry, you hear me? He likes his prizes big and shiny, just like that nose of yours." Now this hits me like a sucker punch, and I can't help myself—I start to laugh. And soon Joe's laughing too. And then he takes a step back and looks at me like a guy he thought he was going to have to bury in the backyard. But we're laughing hard now, like our lives depended on it. And you know what the strange thing is? They do.

Finally, he glances over at the bottle says, "Can I put this away now?"

I tell him, "Yeah, Joe. Put it away."

So he reaches for the bottle, but stops just short of it and puts his hand flat on the table. Then he stands up straight like he just heard a noise and takes a deep breath and brings his eyes halfway across the room to mine, and stops. He looks at the wall like it was me, not a wall, and he says, "Are you done with it, Jim?" And then he finally turns and looks me dead in the eye and says, "Can I throw this fuckin' thing out now? Without you digging through the trash for it tomorrow, that is?"

So I nod my head and say, "Yeah, Joe. You can throw it out. I won't go digging through the trash. I promise."

There's a little something to illustrate what I just said about getting sober not being for the weak of heart. But it's this kind of stuff that wears you out and wears you down. Although, like they say, what doesn't kill you makes you stronger. Obviously, it didn't take me out that time; instead—indeed, I grew stronger, thanks to Joe L. Because the truth is, I didn't have a snowball's chance in hell without him.

So by now, I've finally got the family in my corner—all of them. And that feels good. Of course, being Catholic, they're pushing me to get back together with my wife. Which brings up the big question: Do I love her? I know. All you in the mezzanine want to know. Well, I'm sorry, but that's not the way the story goes this time. I wasn't too clear about it because of all the guilt and remorse I felt over what I'd put her through. Truth is sometimes all that heartache kind of felt like love. But in the back of my mind I knew it wasn't. Not that I knew what love felt like, because I didn't and wouldn't for years and years to come.

But as I said, my folks, being strict Catholics, were pushing hard. So now my father weighs in. Pop doesn't go into action too often, but when he does, watch out! One day he takes me for a walk in the little park near their place and he lets his hair down. He says, "The truth is, Jimmy, there were some mighty lean years in the love department between your mother and me." Which I already know. Where's the Irish family of ten, right? But he goes on to tell me that they stuck it out because that's what man and wife do. And today, he says, it's all he could want it to be. Now I stop in my tracks and look at him hard, and say, "All?" And he looks back at me and says, "All."

Now I talk it over a couple of times with Joe and we go pretty deep with it. In the end, I decide it's worth a shot. So I buy some flowers and I knock on the door of the place right next to the bar where I used to get blotto. Her mother answers the door and she goes pale with her eyes huge, like she's seeing a ghost. Which is what I was to her, I guess. She looks down at the flowers and then back up at me, and she calls, "Patricia," with this totally blank look on her face. Not happy, not sad. Just kind of resigned. Now Pat comes around the corner with a broom in her hand, she takes one look at me, and drops the broom. And then this very pretty, very sad smile creeps over her face. And she steps forward and takes the flowers. Now you up there in the mezzanine can fill in the blanks.

So I get back with my wife and we get on with our lives. It isn't everything it could have been, but what is when you're twenty-eight and just waking up from a sleep deep as old Rip Van Winkle's? But I give it a real try. I go back into the trucking business and put the money on the kitchen table. Not all of it. I have to admit that. I give Pat a check for maybe three-quarters of it and stick the rest in an account of my own. Why? I guess I just needed to know it was there. Just for me. In case things didn't work out. Or maybe it was my disease putting ammo aside for World War III. I don't know exactly why. By this time I'd been out of the trucking business for a number of years because I didn't want to do what I'd done while I was an active alcoholic.

In the rooms they tell you to avoid persons, places, and things that were a big part of your drinking. Sure, they say a lot of crazy stuff in meetings, like, if you started shaving on the right side of your face when you were drinking heavy, in sobriety, start on the left. Crazy stuff like that. Fortunately, my sponsor knows I'm a rebel, that I can only take so much of somebody telling me what to do before I tell them where to go. From the start Joe would take me aside and say, "Forget these guys that want to tell you it's their way or the highway. That you have to do the steps in just this order. Do it cafeteria style, hear me? Load up your tray with what works for today, and leave the rest. It'll still be there tomorrow, and one of these days, the time'll be right and you'll know it. Or if you avoid a step too damn long, I'll sneak it in my glove and knock you cold with it. You trust me by now, right Cusack?" Yes, I did.

So I went back to work in trucking, because it had been five long years already that I hadn't had a real job, and a family has to eat! Were there any kids in this family? No. Sadly, Pat had one miscarriage and that was our only attempt to bring new life into a world that seemed to be in trouble enough as it was.

One morning I'm up finishing a pot of coffee before heading off to work, when I hear this loud *boom* from upstairs. Not a *crash*, not like something falling and breaking. More like a low, heavy thud. Immediately, I have this creepy feeling like I know exactly what it was. I call out, "Pat?" but there's no answer. So I run up the stairs two at a time yelling "Patty? Answer me! Patricia!" When I finally get upstairs—there she is on the floor. Completely paralyzed.

She was like that for six or seven months. I visit her in the hospital three, four times a week. Not that I have the least idea of what to say. When she finally gets out, we move in with my in-laws for a while, in that apartment where I first saw her outside that gin mill I used to go to, where I went back with flowers after we'd been through hell and back. I left her there with her mother and father. I never got along great with my mother-in-law, but the last go around, we tried. Awful as it is to say, it was kind of the same with her beautiful daughter, now paralyzed and speechless. The thing is, we did try, twice. That's the truth. And the fact that we tried and failed to love each other was almost like a kind of love. I know I said that before, but it's true. Maybe it's an Irish thing, I don't know. Sadness is a big part of life, if you're honest with yourself. Right? And when you survive a long stint of sadness with someone you get to be like soldiers who've been through a war together. And for me? It almost felt like love. But almost is only good in horseshoes and hand grenades. It's not the love you hope for from a marriage.

So? What was I supposed to do?

She's paralyzed. She can't talk. She can't do anything. So I'd taken a break of about ten days or so when my father-in-law calls me up and says Pat is back in the hospital and things don't look so good, and maybe I should try to get down there. So I get hold of Joe and we go to see her there in the hospital together. But Pat didn't remember me so well. And she didn't receive me so well, either. It was awkward, to say the least. A couple of days after that, she dies. I mean, I know she's going to. She hasn't gotten any better, only worse. So God took pity on her and took her home. It's like her life was a misery almost from beginning to end. And I was part of the misery. I've got some shame around all that still. Because she was a person who had little or no joy to give or receive, physically, and—of course—I had sensed that. Even if I didn't know it for sure until her father finally tells me, while she's dying. When he takes me out in the hall and tells me she was gang-raped. Then it was like when a door clicks open without even touching it. It all made sense. What I already knew without knowing how I knew. All those years I came around looking for what could only cause her more unhappiness. So now I find out why that is. And then she dies, and part of me feels like a creep because, to tell you the truth—I'm relieved. But another part of me feels like the guy holding the bag. The patsy. The fall guy. Like maybe this "happiness" stuff just isn't in the cards for me. It's just not going to happen for me. And if it's not going to happen, then why bother with all the work of staying sober? Because it's work. Make no mistake about it. And you know what? A couple a days after the funeral, suddenly I'm tired of the work. All this miserable fighting the compulsion and shaving on the other side of my fool face, and for what? For what? For this misery? I don't think so. No, I don't think so. Suddenly, I feel like I'm being played for a sucker. Like I was promised all this serenity, but it's a ripe crock. My wife is dead and buried and I'm clueless what to do next. Until I get this bright idea. And you'll never guess what that is, right? Oh, but I bet you will. That's right, in another minute I'm planning this drunk, of course I am! It seems to come out of nowhere, but actually, it was in the back of my mind the whole time. Like that secret bank account with the passbook taped to the bottom of my top drawer. But so what! I'm entitled to it. Damn right I am! So the plan takes shape like this: I'll take a trip up to the Adirondacks. I have a few bucks in the bank. A new car. So I figure I'll buy a case of whiskey, drive up, and tie a load on in the mountains, and then? Maybe I'll go back to meetings and maybe I won't.

But now I told you to start with that I've got sixty-odd years of uninterrupted sobriety. So some of you are peeking at the cheat sheet and realizing I didn't do it. I didn't "slip," or "go back out," or "pick up," or in plain English, start drinking again. But you've also seen what a stubborn SOB I've been from the age of five when I threw that coat on the floor. So the smart ones among you are wondering what in God's name stopped me—this pathological tough guy—from going on the mother of all benders after his wife finally dies after six months of her lying in bed like a vegetable. What stops him? You want to know. But most of you have already guessed, because there's only one thing that *could* have saved an idiot like me. That's right, I had an angel on my side. Not one in heaven, although with the nine lives I've lived in this my one life, I wouldn't be surprised if I didn't have one or two up there too. I had an Earth angel. You know the guy, a window washer, strapped for years to the ledges of Manhattan's tallest structures, up there with his squeegee and pail thirty, forty, fifty stories up, drunk out of his gourd, too terrified to do the work sober, five days a week. The guy sobered up in meetings lead by Bill W. and Dr. Bob—that's right, the founders of this thing we call AA. You got it. Joe L. His name was Joe Lemon. He's long gone now, and his family, too. If anybody related to him is still on this Earth, they have no reason not to be as proud as can be of the guy. They wanted to put his story in the book that became a bestseller that changed the world. The book called *Alcoholics Anonymous*, which folks in the program call simply *The Big Book*. They wanted to put Joe's story in *The Big Book*, but he wouldn't have it. He said it would swell his head and his sponsees would get the wrong idea, like he was somebody special, when the truth is, as Joe always said, "I'm just a garden-variety drunk." So I'm breaking your anonymity, Joe. And heaven can deal with that, right? Because that's where you are you, no doubt in my mind. Joe Lemon, my sponsor, you were a Twelve-Step genius. Nose like a greyhound, eyes like a hawk, a mind like Sherlock Holmes.

Now, a few days after my wife's funeral Joe calls me up and says, "Let's have coffee." I say, "Okay, how about after eight o'clock?" He says, "No, I feel like getting out of the house. Why not meet for coffee now?" So my eyes go big because it's almost like he's onto me and my plan. But I know that's impossible, so I play it cool and say, "Sure, Joe. Usual place?" And he says, "Great, see you in a half hour." So we meet at this place we've been going to for almost six years now, and we greet each other as we always do, shaking hands like the first time I met the guy, but now—friendly and casual. We're sitting at a corner table and having a cup of coffee when he asks me how I'm feeling.

So I say, "It's a little rough, but I'm getting there okay. I'm okay."

Then without him raising his voice or even narrowing his eyes he says to me, "You're full of crap."

It's only when I start to get huffy and say, "What're you talking about, Joe?" that he gets real serious. Not angry. Just serious. Then he asks me if I remember the first night we met. So I say, "Sure, I do, Joe."

And he says, "Tell me what you remember about that night."

So I told him that I was in bad shape back then and my memory wasn't too clear about that night. Of course, I'm hedging, trying to figure out his game. I tell him I'm not too sure, but I remember that I opened up with him, and that I unloaded a bunch of stuff, that I got some relief from the shame that had been building up for years and years. And I finish with, "Then, of course, we went to the meeting."

Now Joe looks all cool and says, "Of course we did. And that was what? Almost six years ago, right?"

Naturally, I agree. But damn it all if remembering that stuff in the here and now didn't start to bring it all back. Of course, I still have my plan to get drunk. I've made up my mind about that. But all of a sudden it's like . . . how to explain this? It's like I'm a bank robber on his way to a heist who runs into an old pal who became a cop. Suddenly, the bank robber starts to think about what happens when he goes through with the heist. He realizes he may have to shoot his pal—or get shot by him. And suddenly the plan he was so sure of—well, he starts to have second thoughts. And now my stomach is fluttering on me, and it isn't the coffee.

At this point Joe looks at me real careful, sizing me up, still not angry, still cool as a cucumber, when he says, "You know what I remember from that night?" So of course, this way the SOB makes me ask. So I do, and then, he takes a sip of coffee, and looks away a moment, and when he looks back he says it fast and tough: "That first night we met, you told me you didn't care whether or not you were ever going to drink again. In fact, you said you didn't care whether you were ever going to be with your family again. You said you just wanted to get rid of the fears. You didn't say what kind of fears; you just called them 'the fears,' like somehow you thought I'd know what you meant. And I did. I knew what you meant. Because I'd been there. And I shook my head to tell you I understood without interrupting you. So you saw that I understood, and then you repeated yourself, and then you went a little further, like a scared rat coming just a little further out of your rat hole. You said, 'I just want to get rid of the fears and these shakes,' and then you went so far as to hold up your hand for a moment which was shaking like a guy who's got the palsy and a tin cup in his lap where you drop in the nickel. And then you almost teared up when you said, 'I just want to be normal again. I'm not asking for anything but that. I just don't want to be crazy any more. I just want a fresh start, that's all. I don't need any charity—I just don't want to be crazy anymore.'"

Now I'm staring at Joe, who's staring back at me. But he just leaves it like that, the memory of that night hanging in the air. And then he asks me, "Do you remember any of that, Jim?" So I admit I do. And then he says, "Do you think God had anything to do with giving you the courage to fight off going into that gin mill earlier that day? Or do you think you did it all on your own?"

I see where he's going with this, so I throw a tack under his wheels to slow him down when I say, "I go back and forth on that one sometimes, Joe."

"Oh, you do, do you? Well, tell me this. If you had to place a bet on the chances of your walking past that bar that day, what would the odds be of you getting so far as to have your hand on the door of the gin mill, but then pushing it away and walking past it like you did. What do you say the odds of your doing that might have been, Jimmy?"

He never called me Jimmy before, that sneaky bastard—and it was a low punch, all right, the SOB. "What were the odds, Cusack? Come on, you're a gambling man! What were the odds of you walking by like you did that day? Huh? Tell me!"

All of a sudden he's letting me have it, so if only to shut him up, I admit, "A hundred to one, maybe."

He nods, bitterly. "At best, a hundred to one. More like a thousand to one. But leave that for now. So what popped into your head then that helped you pull off those odds and come up a winner? You called somebody. Who was that, again? I don't remember so good."

"Father Parks, and you remember as well as me, you bastard!" I said, smiling as I started to tear up—damn this guy to hell!

"That's right, it was Father Parks. And yeah, he called me up and had me walk away from a Saturday afternoon with my boys to shake the hand of the saddest drunk I ever saw who wasn't blinking up from the gutter on the Bowery. Oh, but you were a proud one. And I'm not ribbing you when I say it. It took guts to do what you did. Real guts. You had to swallow your pride that day, Cusack, instead of a shot of rye—didn't you, Jim? The pride that just about killed you. But instead, somehow the Lord above used a can opener on your heart. And what was the can opener, huh, Cusack? It was me, Jim. It was me. And Christ knows you were a long shot. Oh, my dear sweet Jesus, but were you! A dark horse in a darker race. But so was I, you lousy drunk! So was I! Yet someone sat with me for years, drinking coffee like we've been doing, sharing secrets, neglecting his family and friends. But what friends? Who am I kidding? A guy like me or my sponsor before me? Guys like us don't have any friends. Not the kind people talk about when they use the word. No. I have sponsees now. My family and my sponsees. That's all I have, Jim. And that's all my sponsor had—because he was raised from the dead, pal! Just like I am! Just like you've been for damn near six years. And if you think I can't smell your rotten plan to piss on all that—all the time and work and love I've poured into you—and yes, God has poured into you, you self-pitying piece of—no, I won't say it! Restraint of tongue and pen—that's right," he yelled, quoting scripture. "Restraint of tongue and pen!"

Out of the corner of my eye, I can see people glancing at each other and picking up their cups and saucers, muttering to each other and moving away from us. But I don't dare say a word because I've never seen him like this before, old Joe, not quite. Nor will I ever see him like this again. He's a man on fire. And every word he says is true. So I have to let him have his say. I have to wipe my eyes of tears and just sit there and take it. So take it I do.

"But tell me this, Jim Cusack, you scheming Mick! If God Himself were listening that night you poured *half* your heart out to me—and He was, I assure you, pal, but I don't have no proof—especially if you go back out, then I have less than no proof. And when people say I have a gift? And that my life means something? Sonny boy, if you back out, you are going to rob me of one of few things I have the right to be proud of, which is you, you blockhead. You! Listen, I got two satisfactions in this life as a sober drunk. One is being sober myself, and having the joys of my family and their love and trust brought back into my life. And the other is passing on this gift I got, this gift of sobriety, to guys like you. In hopes that you might do the same someday when I'm out of this for-shit world, and maybe—just maybe onto a better one. But before you make your decision— and sure, it's yours to make—answer me this, and then I'll leave you to do as you decide. But first, tell me this. Okay, Cusack?"

"Okay."

So Joe's like a horse you think has come on too strong, too fast, and the pack is gaining on him when suddenly, from out of God knows where, he pours on strength and speed to leave you speechless.

"Now if God were listening to that sad, proud little speech I just reminded you of, if He were listening that night almost six years ago, and if He found pity in his heart for your sorrow and admiration for your courage—let's just say for argument's sake, He did. And since this horrible world ain't just ruled by Him no more but by our own cockamamie self-will, then Jim, if God were listening to what you said that night, tell me, were any of those requests you made ignored? Were there any of those things you asked for that weren't given to you? Answer me that." And then he the added the word "Please."

So I shook my head no, because I knew I couldn't say the word without losing it. And gentle now he tells me: "Say it aloud, Jim."

So I said, "No, they were all answered."

"Is that right?" Joe says. "You sure about that? When you asked for the fears to be removed, were they?"

"Yeah."

"And then you asked for your hands to stop shaking. And did they?"

"Yeah, they did."

"And then you asked to be released from insanity. And were you?"

I guess maybe I mumbled when I said, "Yeah." Because he said, "I didn't hear you."

"Yeah. I got better. I stopped being a crazy man. I was released from that."

"And now what was the last thing you asked for, Jim?"

"I asked—" and sure, I lose it now, but I say anyway, "I asked to be given another chance at life."

"And do you feel like that request was answered too? Tell the truth."

"I'm not so sure about that one, Joe. My wife is dead, and—"

"That's right, Jim. Your wife is dead. Home with God—and may she find peace in heaven, peace which she never knew down here. Because it was taken from her. And not by you. Get that? Now listen to me," he says, and he places his hand on top of mine just for a second and squeezes it good and hard. And then he lets go and says, "I'm never going to say this again, okay? Unless we need to talk about it, but tell me this—in your heart of hearts, is this the woman you were supposed to go through life with? Huh, Jim? Between you, me, and God above. Was this the woman you were supposed to go through life with?"

Now I take the deepest breath I think I ever took in my life and let it out with the words, "No. May she rest in peace, but . . . no."

"You see where I'm going with this, don't you, pal?" Joe said. "She was miserable here. And couldn't be a proper wife to you, Jim. And God forgive me for saying so, but your last request was granted with things the way they are *now*. You've got another chance at the whole shooting match. Don't you see that? The whole damn thing. And you're a young man yet. Now, it's hard where you are, Jim. And I'm not saying otherwise. And I'm not saying you shouldn't pray at the poor girl's grave, because you should. But do you understand what I'm trying to say to you today?"

"I think I do, Joe. Thanks."

"The real thanks you could give me would be to say something a little different, Jim. Can you imagine what it is that I might just go home a happy man, if you were to say it to me right now?"

"Okay," I say. "I won't do it, Joe."

At this he sighs and looks up and whispers, "Thank you God in heaven." And then he smiles at me with the sweetest,

most totally exhausted smile you ever saw before driving the
last spike into the heart of the devil himself when he asks me,
"You're not going to do what, Jim?"

So I just have to hand it over.

"I'm not going to drink over it," I say. "Okay—it's true, okay?
I had a plan all worked out. I was going to buy a case of booze
and go up to the mountains and . . . But I won't do it. Okay? I
promise, Joe. I promise you I won't! Okay?"

Now it's his turn to tear up, and my turn to smile through
the ones already spilling down my cheeks.

—⚬⚬⚬—

When I left the cemetery where my wife was buried, where I
talked to her for quite a while, and where I said things I should
have said when she was still alive but never did, after all that, I
came back to my in-laws, and my mother-in-law got hold of me
and she said, "Jim, if you're going to go out and drink now, go
out and piss on her grave first."

Then it all fell into place, clear as a church bell ringing in its
tower. I knew Joe had set me up for this, wearing me down so
now this could come sailing in, like the second insurance policy
God gave me that day. Joe gives me the sermon and then my
mother-in-law provides me the bayonet in the heart, the one I
can't ever forget, even if these people are all long gone. "If you're
going to go out and drink now, go out and piss on her grave
first." That's the keeper. I thought I was sure after the talk with
Joe. And I was sure—but then after my Patricia's mother nailed
it like she did, I just said to myself, "So all right. It stays like
this." And you know what? Through good times and bad, it has.

AA entered into my life for real then. I realized I'd just been
dry up to this point, not sober. I had no idea of what the nature
of this disease was all about, this three-fold disease, preying on

mind, body, and spirit. But I finally understood now, and I think that's when I started to grow. That day, I realized there was more to sobriety than just putting down the bottle. I started to get some kind of an idea about what this three-fold disease was all about, and yes, I started to get some benefits. Some freedom inside myself. I started to forgive myself and to look at the value of what the twelve steps of recovery were all about, how I could kind of incorporate them in my life. Before, I'd done it cafeteria style, like Joe told me to, because I was too stubborn to do it any other way. I was ready to go through the steps in order and to reap their rewards, at last.

Five

Maximum Service

S OBRIETY IS A WORLD all by itself, and you get caught up in it and find things to do to help other people do what you're trying to do, which is get a whole new shot at life. First off, I'm one of the only guys going to meetings who has a car. And not one of these pieces of junk that's always in the shop. I mean a brand new 1954 Buick two-door, with a simonize. So guys who've lost everything—like I had—they look up and see a sober alcoholic can get his life back. Before long I've become like a chauffeur service. I'm picking up alcoholics off the street, buying them a cup of coffee, and taking them to meetings all over the place. I go to prisons and hospitals and speaker's meetings where I share my "experience, strength, and hope." But remember when my pop punched out Pete Cowboy? And the way I took that force for good and went overboard with it, fighting, but not the good fight? No, it was more like I'd fight any fight. Well, here it's happening again. I'm taking the life-saving message of our Twelve-Step Program and going overboard with it—getting to feel like I'm quite the big shot. And my sponsor knows it. Joe saved my life bringing me into the program, but he can't teach me humility. That one's between me and my Higher Power.

There was this gay guy trying to get sober who I helped out when I could. We used to grab a coffee before I'd drive him to a meeting. He was honest and smart, too—maybe too smart. They say sometimes it's the guys with all the brains that don't get it because they can't open up without some written invitation. But this particular fellow had some real guts, and maybe that was important for me to see.

One time, I picked up this bunch of guys at this coffee shop in Queens. The car is full and we're about to take off when suddenly this gay guy runs up, all out of breath, and says he needs to get to a meeting. So I look behind me, even though I know we're full, and I see these tough guys staring at me as if to say, "You're not going to make us stick four back here with him, are you?" Now, deep inside I know I should tell them to shove over and make room in the back for one more. But I chicken out. Instead of being a stand-up guy for a fellow recovering alcoholic, I say, "Sorry pal, we're full up. I'll get you over there tomorrow, but be on time!" And with that we drive off like a bunch of sober tough guys.

That night his mother calls me and says she got my number out of her son's pocket. That he hung himself a few hours ago, and that he had my number in his pocket when she found him.

Now that one kind of woke me up for a minute or two. Today it's something I've learned to live with, that I "coulda woulda shoulda" done different. But life only comes over the plate at you this once. No rehearsals. It's all live, like the early TV shows coming up all over the place now, Jack Parr and Jackie Gleason. But life is in color, not black and white. And the ones that die in the show don't get up before the credits and take a bow, like in fancy theaters. At least not here on Earth.

Sometimes I drive a bunch of sober alcoholics to picnics and dances where maybe we can meet somebody with "some time"—which in program lingo means some time sober—the idea being that single people with good recovery hook up and help each other stay sober while exploring the earthly love most of us need. Well, that's sort of what happened to me, but it was a little different than that, actually. I met my second wife in the rooms, but she wasn't an alcoholic. She was there supporting a family member.

My second wife's name was Millie. She was twelve years older than me and had three kids from a previous marriage. We became good friends. And I was a good stepfather to her kids. I don't know how much I really loved her, or how much I was actually capable of real intimacy and true love back then. The thing is, we were good to each other and good for each other. And I'd never known a relationship like that. The only negative was that she wasn't religious, so we just got married at the justice of the peace, and soon I stopped going to church altogether. I guess, at the time, it felt like our Twelve-Step Program was all the spiritual life I needed.

Millie and the kids and I moved up to Orange County. I bought a nice house in Middletown for $8,000. I'm making good money driving for the Teamsters and running around helping people in the program—and Millie's fine with that. So time rushes by like it does. One of those mileposts on the highway of life we all look back on is the assassination of JFK. And maybe it's important to check in with a few of those posts because recovery can become like a bubble that floats up and doesn't have anything hardly to do with the rest of the world. But the work we do is with and for the rest of the world, as well as for the good of our souls and our own spiritual health.

So back on that terrible day I was trucking hard and heavy, putting in the hours. Fact is, I loved it. Driving all hours of the day and night. Hanging out with tough guys who put in the same kind of hours, taking the same kind of risks—falling asleep at the wheel, blowing out a tire at high speed, keeping an eye out for the truck-jacker with a Blackjack in their back pocket, that kind of thing. Well, I pulled up to a stop sign in front of a warehouse I'd loaded up, and I see this black guy who loads trucks there. We'd become friends, and I wave at him, but he doesn't wave back. I look closer, and these tears are just flowing down his face. I jump out of the truck, and before I get out the question, he blurts, "They slain the president." The word "slain" struck me as being like something out of the Bible, like a king of Egypt killed or a saint in his martyrdom. So the world crashed down that day. I called my parents, who'd worshipped JFK. We hadn't spoken for nine years, since I got married outside the church. And then? Life rolls on.

Now, the twist in the tale goes like this: I get a dog, I forget where. A big, handsome German Shepherd I name Jake. Jake is fine when I'm around to reassure people about him (and to reassure Jake about people), but when I'm not around he gets surly and snappy, and before long, he bites somebody. And then it happens again. So I know I have to put him down. But I get all upside-down about this. It really upsets me. So I drive around talking to this mutt who can't keep his jaws off people. Maybe he reminds me a little of me, back in my dark times. But the world doesn't have any Twelve-Step program for a dog that bites. So I'm driving around, having a couple last good times that he doesn't know are the last good times. Maybe I even think about a drink once or twice. I'm pretty down in the dumps, but I make the appointment with the vet and do what has to be done. Then I drive up the thruway to get it off my mind. I like to drive—always have. But this isn't working, either. So I pull off the thruway and start driving in the country. I see a place where I can stop and get some coffee. So I order my coffee and this guy comes over and says, "Looks like you could use a friend. Mind if I sit down?"

I say, "No, I don't mind," and soon I explain where I'm at, and he listens, and then he points at me says, "Why don't you go over to Auriesville to the Shrine of the North American Martyrs. It's just a couple of miles up the road. That's one place a guy can find some peace." So I shake his hand, and as I thank him, I have a funny feeling he might be from the program, but I don't ask. Instead, I get back in behind the wheel.

Auriesville turns out to be the place where two French Missionaries were killed by the Mohawks they were trying to convert to Catholicism in the mid-sixteen hundreds. A third monk escaped and returned years later and tried to convert the Mohawks all over again, only to be killed by the same men that had killed his brothers. Hundreds of years later all three of these Jesuit Brothers are canonized and their shrine is blessed by the Pope. The whole trip feels weird because it begins with my having to put Jake down, which kind of opened up this hole. And I'd been feeling like maybe I was going through the motions and needed a new direction in my life. I was married to a good woman, but to tell you truth, I missed taking Holy Communion and that feeling of getting right with God. Now suddenly, after this series of coincidences, I'm kneeling at a Catholic shrine, asking for direction from the God of my fathers for the first time since I couldn't remember when. And driving away I felt lighter somehow, like my prayers had been heard.

Not even two weeks later I got a call from a guy I knew from my home group in Middletown, asking me if I was interested in maybe putting a detox center back on its feet. When I heard this a shiver ran up my spine.

Back then, in the early 1960s, detoxes were extremely few and far between. There were a couple of famous ones in the Midwest. One was called Hazel's Den and was run by a recovered alcoholic by the name of Pat Butler and his wife. That became Hazelden. So Hazelden, along with a place run by Carol and Dick Caron called Chit Chat (years later called The Caron Foundation), these were the pioneers. They were Twelve-Step based and run with real heart—the best we had. Of course, you also had your psychiatric hospitals, what the first wave of sober alcoholics sometimes called "flight decks." The expensive ones were almost like resorts with bars on the windows and nurses instead of maids. But the state-run ones—well, those were pretty rough. There was a movie back then called *The Snake Pit*, which was a horror movie almost, about a woman's psychiatric hospital which became known as hell on Earth. And I've already told you about Kings County for the criminally insane. That was about the toughest place I'd ever seen—and I've seen some bad ones. In fact, Kings County is the one place I couldn't bring myself to go back to and speak at a meeting. I just couldn't stomach it. But maybe the most shocking part about "the early days" is, you couldn't get a hospital to detox an alcoholic. They'd say, "Take them to church or the psych ward, or bring them back to their families, or drop them off at the bowery where they'll end up sooner or later anyway—but get them out of here!" Occasionally, you'd have a hospital, a place like Mount Carmel Guild, that would provide a detox—theirs in reality was little more than a warehouse with a padlock on the door where alcoholics were left to their own shaking, sweating, hallucination-soaked hell. And when these individuals got out? Alcoholics were on their own. It was sink or swim. And the statistics for such "hard cases" actually staying sober after drying out were practically hopeless, by which I mean less than a hundred to one.

You remember the candy store my folks had? Where I got into trouble with gambling and taking bets? Well, once I finally "got it," that candy store became a different kind of hot shop. There were a few of us—the second wave, you might say—alcoholics who met Bill W. in a meeting or two as I did but who were basically brought back to life by the Earth angels he and Dr. Bob got sober, guys like Joe Lemon or those who allowed their stories to be written up in *The Big Book*. Another important figure in the second wave was a guy named Mickey Diamond—who you'll hear about more later. People say they can hear the street in my voice when they talk to me, that I haven't forgotten where I come from. Well, if you can hear the street in my speech, you can hear the subways *under* the street when you talk to Mickey Diamond. Mickey was one of these guys saved by the grace of God who hit back at the devil so hard he lost his wife and seven kids because the program put them in the shadows. All he ever thought about was how to save the next suffering alcoholic. So Mickey would bring me guys at the candy store—hard cases—and we'd take turns in the back room babysitting these alcoholics as they sweated out their demons. We'd give them a shot and six hours later maybe another one, and six hours after that maybe a half shot—and then they'd get no more from us. Then it was between an alcoholic and his own Higher Power, "May you find Him now!" as it says in the literature.

One of these guys Mickey brought into the candy shop didn't make it. He didn't die where I could see him—but I sat there with him, spelling Mickey while this drunk shook and shivered. A few days later Mickey told me the guy was dead. And it scared me, I don't mind admitting that. But this is life and death we're talking about here. I knew that from my own battle. And now I knew it again here, but the coin toss didn't up end heads. It was tails this time. An alcoholic was dead. You fought for him but you could lose the battle. In fact—you did lose the battle, occasionally. And not just once. But you had to protect yourself so you survived to help another more fortunate one the next time around.

Sure, I dried out a few alcoholics on the couch in the back room of my parents' candy store. But all that went to my head. I'd been the big shot back then, one that needed to find some humility before my Higher Power was ready to help me bring it to the next level. So now maybe you have a better idea why a shiver ran up my spine when this friend from my home group called about a detox in trouble. Because if you've come this far, you know that I'd been a textbook case of a total down-and-outer—and I'd made it back. That's what I prayed for back at Auriesville—for a new direction, a better relationship with God, and a way to help down here on Earth. And here was the answer to that prayer.

Glen Acre Lodge was a little more than an hour away, near Port Jervis in Sullivan County. It was a big old lodge that needed a fair amount of work, and though I tried to keep it to myself, I thought it was the most beautiful thing I ever saw. The guy running it had taken off somewhere. His wife was left with four kids and didn't know the first thing about running a detox, so sure enough, it fell on hard times. But the basic structure was still good. The roof didn't sag too badly which, as my uncles taught me, is the first thing you look at in a building. There were two drying-out rooms in the back which were connected to each other, a living room, two dining rooms, two bathrooms, a couple of kitchens, another room with a TV, a rec room with a Ping-Pong table, a separate two-car garage. And hanging over this whole setup was a huge house of twenty little bedrooms with a wing in the back of fifteen more.

My friend and I sat down with the owner and made a list of the bills and taxes owed, which were considerable. On top of that, the place needed a bunch of cosmetic repairs, most of which I could handle. "I wouldn't be able to pay you anything," the owner—a woman by the name of Doris—said, sounding pretty hopeless. "Not until the place climbs back into the black, which could take—"

"Maybe three months," I said, interrupting her. "Not including a couple spent fixing her up to start with."

"Oh, well," she said, "who would ever volunteer for that?"

"I would," I said. And she blinked and sat up straight as my friend began to laugh.

Of course, Millie thought I was crazy. But I'd worked hard in trucking and put some money away. To me it seemed pretty clear. I had prayed for a new direction in life and this was what rolled down the chute. So I'm fine with it, and I sign on with no guarantees. Luck seems to be on my side, and as a matter of fact, things are moving ahead of schedule. Until, that is, I'm working on the place late one night and a couple of cars roll up, and five guys step out, pretty liquored up. Two of them are almost my size. They've all got bottles in their hands, except for two guys with knives. Now I'd heard about some lowlifes who'd ended up running the detox before the state padlocked the door, so I have a pretty good idea who these clowns are. As a matter of fact, I'm almost surprised they haven't shown up sooner.

"I'm not open for business yet," I yell—not too friendly, standing in the door. They kind of mumble a few swears, so I take a step towards them and suggest, "Why don't you guys go sober up somewhere else? I'm in no mood for company. You got that?"

"You're the chump," one of the bigger guys says, "trying to take over our business."

"Wasn't any business left to take!" I say, and maybe I spit on the ground. "Not the way you were running things. Taking money from desperate people trying to dry out a drunk. But you didn't dry him out so good, did you? Not the way I heard it. Now get out of here."

They hesitate like a pack of snarling dogs, then start towards me, but not too quick. I move fast into the house and come back out with a Babe Ruth slugger I'd brought along on a hunch. So I do a little batting practice and connect a couple of times.

Not with any skulls, thank God. But they back off fast, yelling and swearing, start up their cars, and peel off down the country road. And I never see one of them again.

⸞⸡

A Dr. Petkus from over the line in Pennsylvania is kind enough to drop in several times a week to check on my first clients. He assesses the guys I've knocked out for a few hours with what I call the Glen Acre Cocktail. It's down the hatch and then goodnight, Irene. They wake up eight to twelve hours later and the real fun begins. You never know what you're going to get with the DTs, but the most important thing is to always play along. If it's a chicken coop they see, fine; I'll pick up the mother hen, take a few eggs for breakfast, put her back down. And then ask the client, "You want them scrambled or fried?" He looks at me really carefully to make sure I'm not messing with his head, and then he says, "Scrambled, with ketchup. No, wait a minute. I'm not hungry right now. Maybe later. Where's that rooster hiding? You have to be careful with him."

"Can't be too careful of that damn rooster!" I agree. "Nasty bastard!"

"You're telling me! I have scars to prove it!"

"Did you grow up on a farm? A city boy like you?" This way I get his trust. Right there in the middle of Crazy Land.

Then when he comes out of it he might say to me, "You didn't really see no hens in there, did ya?"

And I'll say, "No, for me it was a delivery boy I greeted at the door with a knife in my hand. Tell you the truth, I like your hallucination better."

And before you know it, we're laughing together—one alcoholic with another. And we've started to open the double doors of recovery at the Glen Acre Lodge.

Soon I've got Jo heading the women's wing and Ralph for a cook. He's no kid, so I let him sleep in most mornings. I cook breakfast myself for the whole place and run a meeting right after, unless, of course, I'm sweating out the DTs with a new client, in which case Ralph handles the spatula, and the meeting waits a little while. Come afternoon, I walk a bunch of newly sober individuals down to Hattie's, the local candy store. They get a lot of business from us. At this stage in the evolution of "the recovery movement," a chocolate bar or two is always in the pocket or purse of anybody trying to get off the sauce. In the evening I'll shuttle a bunch over to Honesdale, Pennsylvania, for a meeting. Soon we have meetings swing through and visit us. But I run a tight ship. There's no fraternizing between men and women that is not strictly supervised. This love stuff is strong medicine for good or ill—and it's a terrible distraction for someone who needs to look long and hard at themselves.

In the beginning, Doris and her kids were still living at the lodge. Eventually, they got a little place just down the road, but to begin with it was a bit of a madhouse, everything happening at once—everything, that is, except me getting much in the way of sleep. The biggest problem was that I had a hard time getting back to see Millie and the kids. But what could I do? Not only was this a more than full-time job, but I was doing the work I loved, figuring out how an alcoholic could get sober and stay sober. And yet—as I said earlier—this was different from AA. People were being brought here through intervention, against their will, which is counter to AA's philosophy, then walking out and starting up a meeting wherever it is they call home. They come in as prisoners of war and they walk out fighting the good fight. Or trying. It's true, I felt like maybe I was a foot soldier in a revolution.

In our Program you're called a "recovering" alcoholic even if you have fifty years sober. It's a humility factor built right in—another way of saying "we're all just one drink away from where we were." In the rooms, adding this "-ing" after "recover" is fine. Out in the civilian world, and even more so when you're committed to recovery as a career, you describe yourself more often as a "recovered" alcoholic. Because when people place themselves or are placed in your care, you need to convey a sense of a lifelong commitment to sobriety which the word "recovering" doesn't accomplish as well. I straddle the fence on this one. When I took over Glen Acre Lodge, I was fourteen years sober, and in my heart I felt certain I wouldn't take another drink in this life. But I still say by the grace of God I'm sober "one day at a time."

This commitment, this mission I'm on, was all-consuming then and remains so today. In our Program it's said that a sober alcoholic has to be more careful than a "civilian" about self-esteem issues. The reasons for this, from a clinical point of view, are pretty simple. Even though alcoholics have endured some of the more hideous experiences you'll ever hear about, as they recover we often find them to be particularly sensitive to criticism due to their own private sense of shame. What an irony! Human beings who have lowered themselves to a state not far from that of an animal are often more childlike and sensitive to the hurtfulness of the world than "normal" people, who are less likely to descend into a hell on Earth, and likewise, more likely to crawl up and out of such a miserable state.

After the first five horrendous years off alcohol I hope you've seen me slowly, painfully evolve—perhaps even demonstrate one of our Program's famous promises, "finding that God has done for us what we could not do for ourselves." But my marriage suffered from this almost evangelical mission I was on. I can't tell you exactly when the shift occurred. The fact is, my marriage with Millie died on the vine because I wasn't on hand to nurture it; and for reasons that maybe had as much to do with career as with romantic inclination, I divorced Millie and married Doris, became the co-owner of Glen Acre Lodge, and inherited another wonderful bunch of kids—children of my own being the one blessing I'd never know in this life.

So I overcame some challenges, I was making a real reputation for the Glen Acre Lodge, and doing what I loved to do. But it wasn't all "up, up, and away" like a hit song of that era suggested.

A guy I knew as a friend in the program came in. I gave him the Glen Acre Cocktail, and he went out like a light, fine. But when he came to, he became convinced I was a Japanese general and we were still at war. It sounds like a comedy routine, but he meant business. He came at me all of a sudden, but this was one hallucination I wasn't signing up for. I dodged him once and warned him not to mess around. Then when he came at me again I decked him. I thought, "Hold on, this is not in the playbook. Get a hold of yourself, Jim." When he came to again, I apologized a couple of times, and I thought we were back on a good footing. Then a couple of hours later we were having coffee, and I asked him how he was feeling, and he told me to perform an unnatural act on myself. So—I can't believe I have to admit this but—I decked him again.

That night I called my sponsor down in Queens and told him the story. I said, "I'm not sure I'm cut out for this, Joe. I feel like I'm in over my head. Maybe I'm in the wrong racket and I should go back to trucking."

He told me not to overreact. "After all, he isn't the first guy you hit sober, Jim." Then Joe proceeded to remind me of the time I punched out a drunk who took a swing at me when I was speaking at a BEGINNER'S MEETING in Brooklyn years back, and then he went to the punch line again: "This isn't the first guy you ever hit sober, Jim!" I reluctantly gave in and began to laugh with this wonderful man, and it loosened me up. "You've been doing great work!" Joe told me. The problem, he explained, was taking on a friend and never establishing a professional relationship to begin with. He said, "Don't throw the baby out with the bathwater! You need a break, and you need to find some people you admire to take some advice from, maybe folks to model yourself after."

There was no other place to go but out to Hazelden. We were doing okay money-wise. So I cut back on the intakes and left a skeleton crew to handle what guests were already settled in, and I flew out to Minnesota to look this thing in the eye. I was shaken, all right, and humbled. So I wasn't really prepared for the encouragement awaiting me there.

Maybe you've heard about scientists making the same discovery almost within weeks of each other? Well, imagine my surprise when I arrive a thousand miles away and find that these good people at Hazelden, Pat Butler, his wife, and his crew of recovered alcoholics, are doing exactly what I've been doing without any of us having anything but a vague knowledge of each other. But they've been at it a little longer, so the kinks have been rolled out of the wire better; and sure, Butler is probably getting a little more sleep than I'd been getting for the last year or two. But not much more! He was a general in the revolution I was talking about.

One of the things Butler told me that really hit home and has been an inspiration to me ever since was that "no less than 80% of the recovery process in an alcoholic who makes it in the world outside is gained from within the fellowship they experience—often this first time round." That means person to person. Eyeball to eyeball. Sober alcoholic to wannabe sober alcoholic. Now, in a rehab situation, that "fellowship" is a version of the Twelve-Step program which has been bulked up—because we can't wait for the suffering drunk to come to us. Which means that what I say and do will have to be proof that this strange-sounding stuff actually works. I knew there was only one way to accomplish this, which is to speak from the heart about the darkness—the fear and rage and shame—but to also speak about the light waiting at the end of that terrible black night. And yes, to control my temper. So I vowed to do all that, and to the best of my abilities, that's a vow I've kept.

The fact is, it didn't take me much more than four days of visiting with these wonderful people to realize that my sponsor had been right again. I *was* on the right track—and I needed to get back on the horse which had thrown me. So I flew back to New York and drove up to Glen Acre Lodge with a smile on my face and a new sense of urgency. Okay, I don't want to preach, but I have to say I felt then that the Butlers and the Carons and me and a few others, well, we were all tuned into the same frequency. We weren't many, but we were true believers, all right—all of us on the same mission. There were thousands and thousands of suffering alcoholics in America who needed what we were trying to give them. So I rolled up my sleeves and hung up my sign on the hook above the door again. We were back in business, and I had a fire in the belly, I did. And, like the awful fire I told you about that could sneak underground and pop up all over the place, that hellfire which seemed to surround me back when I was drinking, well, this fire-for-good seemed to go underground and pop up in the strangest places, too, but it was a righteous blaze. My temper was "tempered," my head was finally "right-sized," and I was fighting the good fight. What more could a sober alcoholic ask for?

Six

Induced Therapeutic Surrender

I'VE BEEN STRESSING the importance of the recovered alcoholic and/or addict turning around and extending a hand to those still suffering, confused, and in danger. Certainly, there's no doubt in my mind about the truth of the phrase "It's in the giving that you receive." Nor are these words only true in recovery. They're true in all aspects of life as long as we live it. But I think I've been unfair in not mentioning the contribution of people lucky enough to be born *without* a predisposition towards addiction. The fact is, such individuals have made a huge contribution to the world of recovery, and I don't want to leave them out of this story.

For instance, it was the automobile industry which first made an important discovery about alcohol abuse. Mind you, it was "bean counters" who made this breakthrough—guys in suits trying to figure out how to make a better profit for the home team. So these accountants, or the researchers working for them, figured out that cars rolling off the assembly line built on Mondays and Fridays (as compared to cars completed on Tuesday, Wednesday, and Thursday) required on average about a thousand bucks each in recall dollars to rebuild to the industry standard. And the reason that Monday's and Friday's cars were so poorly built—it was pretty easy to figure—was that the weekend party was both starting early and going late. Monday's cars, completed by workers recovering from hangovers, naturally were the worst of the bunch.

So the CEOs in Detroit realized it would save money to go into the workforce and "encourage" rehabilitation. And how did they do that? By telling a guy with a lousy record that his salary would be covered while he dried out, but that if he chose to disregard this generous offer, he could look for another job— without any recommendation from his present employer. You can bet the unions and the insurance companies got involved pretty quickly, and I'll get to that part of the deal a little later.

Around 1965, I got a call at Glen Acre Lodge from some cops I had gotten sober with back in Green Point, Brooklyn, along with Mickey Diamond and a dozen other heart-of-gold characters. For sure, that was a tough bunch of guys in that meeting, and we did a lot of sharing from the heart. So these buddies of mine, who happened to wear badges for the NYPD, they knew a lot about me, like that my father was big in the Teamsters, that I come from an Irish neighborhood, and that I brushed up against organized crime now and again. Maybe they noticed I know how to say what I need to say to stay sober without running my mouth about stuff that's none of my business. The fact is, by the time I got this call, Glen Acre Lodge had a straight-up reputation. Remember, it's a small world back then, this community of sober alcoholics. People know I run a tight ship, there's no shenanigans with the money or with men and women confusing romance with recovery. No newspaper reporters or photographers come through the door. Or if they ever try . . . let's just say they never try again.

So these friends of mine in the NYPD get me on the phone, and first they congratulate me. But it's not BS, it's real and true: "We've been hearing great things about the Lodge," and "Jim, you've come a long way." The kind of praise that it's probably taken me these fifteen years of sobriety to be man enough to accept at all. Then they tell me the police chaplain, Monsignor Dunne, has been looking at some recent flare-ups in the NYPD around drinking, a couple of cops need to go away a while—keep their pictures out of the paper—get their lives back together. Did I think I could help? I said I'd be honored to try. These cops were some tough customers, my friends explained, and chances are they'd just be brought up without a whole lot of explanations, dried out at Mount Carmel, and then driven straight up to me. Did I think I could handle that? Well, I knew what that meant, all right. So maybe I hesitated a second. Maybe they heard that hesitation so they offered some police backup, and it's possible I was being arrogant like back in the dry days when I said, "Let's see how I do alone." Either way, that's what I said and that's how it went. I don't think I was being arrogant, though. I think I knew it was a solo job. The kind of split-second decisions I'd be making you could never make with another guy unless he was your twin brother, and I didn't have a twin—thank God! This world had quite enough to put up with having just the one of me! They said I'd get paid by the Police Benevolent Association, not by an insurance company. This kind of thing had never been done before, and we needed to proceed on a case-by-case basis. I said I understood. To which they responded, "So how about Friday?"

The first guys came as scheduled. Priority number one was making sure my own head didn't get caved in. Number two was trying to find some common ground. That wasn't easy when a guy has just come through the DTs in a five-day lockdown at Mount Carmel and they think they're on their way home, but instead of going back over the George Washington Bridge from the New Jersey side, the NYPD van they're in "escorts" them up Route 17 to me. I can't say this is exactly what came out of my mouth. It probably wasn't this polite. But it's close.

"I'm sorry you're not home with your wife and kids. Something that happened while you were drinking has a lot to do with why. Can we agree on that? No? Okay, we'll come back to that. In most other cities in this country chances are you'd be talking to your lawyer instead of me because you'd be facing criminal charges. That's right, you'd be behind bars instead of being here. And the fact is, right now, I'm the only thing between you and, at best, losing your job. So you're getting a break. A real break. Why? I guess it has something to do with a sense of brotherhood among the NYPD, even at the top. Fact is, the commissioner is maybe taking some real heat this very moment for protecting you like this. That's right, protecting you. Why? Because of something that happened about a week ago while you were under the influence of alcohol. Now can we agree on that, or do you want to just kiss your job good-bye and take your chances with the district attorney's office?"

In the end, we usually agreed that drinking was the reason they were talking to me. Having established this much, I told them about the way I drank, and then I asked them to tell me about the way they drank. I swore on my mother's life I'd never tell another soul what it was they said. Most of the time guys like these got around to admitting that their drinking had become unmanageable and it was interfering with decision making while they were armed and fulfilling the responsibilities of one of the most dangerous jobs in the world.

So the importance of that mission I realized I was on, that mission of "forcing sobriety upon an alcoholic in denial," was suddenly multiplied by ten. Because this wasn't a civilian accustomed to being told what to do. These were cops who were the ones accustomed to doing the telling. How did that make me feel? I was honored, nervous, and excited as hell. If I thought about it too long I'd realize I was riding the tip of the wave of recovery. It felt like a tidal wave sometimes, one that could smash me to bits. But like everything in this crazy world, when you really look at it, it's all just one day at time. "Because all I have is today." Amen.

Eventually, it wasn't such a surprise anymore: A cop has a problem. He's sent to us for help. Sometimes one is forcibly picked up by his own people; but if a cop had gotten himself into some real trouble, he soon realized that getting away from the photographers of *The Daily News* wasn't such a bad idea. Getting sober? Maybe that would take a while.

They'd heard about "The Farm" by now, which is what the cops had started to call Glen Acre Lodge. In fact, we had to convince a few true believers not to try to make converts on the force. Because that invariably works against us. Nothing worse than the recently reformed to make an enemy of all their old cronies still waist-high in addiction.

Not that starting out was ever easy.

"I don't have a drinking problem!"

How many times have I heard that one? No, it was his birthday and he got a little carried away. Or it was Saint Paddy's Day, or a brother-in-law died suddenly, or he needed to bury the hatchet with so-and-so because of such-and-such, when who walks into the bar but the union guy. "Just my luck!"

No, and you'd never guess most of these cops had just sweated out the DTs at Mount Carmel. No, you didn't hear a word about that. But here I am. I've seated the guy down across the desk from me to get the whole story. I just sort of take in this human being in front of me, try to see things through his eyes at the same time that I'm keeping in my mind my own agenda. Whatever he says happened is what I say happened.

"So if I understand what you're saying to me correctly," I say, staring straight at the guy, "you shouldn't be here at all!"

"That's exactly right!" he says. "You hit the nail on the head!"

"Well, then wait a minute," I say, taking out my phonebook, "listen, I got only so many beds here, and there are some guys out there in real trouble. Not like you! It's clear as the nose on

my face this is all a mistake. Listen, you sit back while I call up
the top brass and get to the bottom of this."

Nine times out of ten the cop reaches out and puts his hand
on the phone so I don't pick it up.

"Wait a minute," he says. "Maybe there is some truth to their
side of it. Maybe I did screw up a couple times."

"Oh!" I say, sounding surprised. "Well, tell you what. Nothing
you say to me leaves this room. So how about we make a deal?
How about you tell me what really happened, okay? And we'll
just take a look at it. Okay? If it's not a problem, I'll get you
out of here. And if it is a problem, what a coincidence! I just so
happen to run a place where a guy can get his life back together.
Because once in a while even a tough guy goes too far and just
has to take a time-out and look at his life, you know? Maybe
make a change for the better. It's hard—takes guts—to make a
real change. But every once in a while a guy with real guts shows
up, steps up to the plate, and takes a mighty swing for the good.
Am I making any sense?"

So that's the way I did it back then, and that's the way I
do it now. No difference. Pills, powders, needles, uppers,
downers, whiskey, wine, stuff that costs two hundred bucks a
bottle—all the same: Put a can opener to the tin, open them
up, and get ready for a real mess. Because that's what is inside
every human being.

—oooo—

Maybe you know me well enough by now to know that I don't
sit around much. And when I do, I'm rolling things around in
my head, praying for guidance, and searching for new ways to
try to win this battle we're in. The thing I was pushing hardest
for those days was getting the families involved. On Sundays,
for instance, the Lodge became an open house with extra food

and coffee and snacks. Now this was for "civilian" families, mind you, not the families of cops. "The blue line" has proven difficult to penetrate, but in civilian recovery programs, wives of newly sober alcoholics have bonded. We encouraged Al-Anon groups to come in and support the spouses of alcoholic clients. Of course, we didn't yet have ACOA (Adult Children of Alcoholics), but we were pushing in that direction from the start. With our Twelve-Step Program, you should understand, alcoholics are made to feel they're in the driver's seat. As you saw in my case, revelations and new understandings come with time, and members, though advised, are given a comfort zone inside which they're "allowed their process"—with the result that the whole story doesn't necessarily come out all at once. But because it was my job to accelerate this process, I was now pushing hard for family counseling, since—in my experience—the real healing only takes place when all sides of the family dynamic are on the table.

Ever notice that when you're trying something totally new, insiders watch and wait for a while? Then if your reputation holds up, they send some work your way and see how you do with it. If you do well, one day you get a call from Mr. Big, who in this case was Monsignor Dunne, the chaplain of the NYPD.

Earlier in life Joseph Dunne had been a chaplain in the 101st Airborne, the paratrooper outfit that dropped into Normandy the night before the D-Day invasion. It was cloudy as hell that night and the jump was off target, and a lot of those paratroopers drowned, died in "short drops," or got hung up in trees. Dunne jumped with them and was there administering last rites to his boys when they needed him most. He was something of a living legend, and he'd been calling the shots in my operation for a year or two before, on this particular day, he reaches out. So I'm sort of expecting this call, hoping for it, nervous about it. But when it finally comes he puts me at ease, congratulating me on the job I'm doing. Then he says he'd like to come up for a visit. "Anytime, Monsignor," I answer, "we'd be honored."

So we arrange for him to come up on a Thursday, midmorning, before I get a fresh load of recruits from Mount Carmel. They arrive in an unmarked car, just him and a plainclothes driver. The monsignor says he wants me to go on with the day like he wasn't there. So I lead a meeting, then we have some lunch. We're talking with some dried-out cops together, then he speaks with one or two in private. So the guys are feeling the loving care of their chaplain, rough and tough though that love may be. The monsignor even joins us for a walk down to Hattie's candy store where he's friendly and free with his praise. On the way, we two slow a little and the flock gets a bit ahead of us. Monsignor Dunne tells me he's studying for another PhD, and his final paper is about the work we're doing together up here at the Lodge. "And do you know what I call what we're doing, Jim?"

I say, "No, Monsignor, tell me."

So he says, "Induced therapeutic surrender. What do you think of that?"

I'm smiling so hard I'm afraid the NYPD's chaplain will take it the wrong way. "I think you got yourself a winner, Monsignor. I think you hit the nail on the head." This way we help addicts get into recovery is now widely known as intervention.

Over the next few months we talk a lot over the phone. He says he'd like me to meet some of the union organizers for the NYPD. These are the guys who've been doing their research, watching the cops who call in sick on Monday on a regular basis, are notorious on Saint Paddy's Day, crash the patrol car too often, have been known to threaten a fellow officer—this kind of thing. By now they're collaring some of these cops in trouble before there's blood on the ground. I've gotten to know several of these union guys pretty well over the phone. A couple of them have even come up to visit, and that makes the cops in recovery feel like the higher-ups are in their corner. So it's good all around. But I haven't gotten down to meet the whole bunch of these union guys because it's hard to leave the Lodge even for an hour, let alone an afternoon. Now, the monsignor knows I'm frustrated with induced therapeutic surrender because it doesn't involve the families. One day in particular I get pretty worked up about it over the phone. So he hears me out and then he starts to tell to me about politics.

"There isn't any politics in heaven, Jim—and tell me why?"

"Because God's in charge up there and doesn't tolerate any monkey business."

"That's exactly right. But there's a hell of a lot of politics down here on Earth, as you know, especially when the unions get involved."

I try to make my point, but he cuts me off. And then he says it, almost tenderly, because maybe he knows I'm right. Even so he says, "I'm telling you, Jim, as a friend. It won't fly."

But I won't quit. "I'm going to make it fly, Monsignor. If you could set up a meeting with all these union heads . . . any day but Friday. If you could do that, I'd be in your debt."

So he sets up a meeting and I bring in a friend who's been around to spell me for the day at Glen Acre. I drive down, and we're in Room 615 of the police station where Monsignor Dunne holds court. There are eight or ten guys assembled, and we shake hands and make some small talk about a few success stories and a recent nightmare.

Then I clear my throat and say, "What an honor it is to be here and to meet you guys because we've all pulled together to help the boys in blue. And we've made some real progress. But there's something really important missing in the approach.

And that is the family input, which is the whole story, and—in my experience—it's only the whole story that gets a guy sober and keeps him that way."

"Don't get me wrong," I continue, "I owe my life to our Twelve-Step Program, but in the rooms the alcoholic calls the shots. He decides what gets shared in a meeting and what gets left out. The upshot is that the guy doesn't have to come clean, and so he's got angers and shames and resentments and this whole closet full of skeletons doing a Halloween dance in his brain, and so a lot of the time he can't get sober. And I want him sober," I say to them. "And so do you."

"So I'm asking you please to send up the families so we can get all the cards on the table. Because then—and only then—we have a real chance at healing some terrible wounds and reuniting these families, and winning this battle one man at a time."

By now the union guys are rolling their eyes and muttering to each other. So the big cheese jumps in and says, "You've done good work, Cusack. You know how to talk with us, and you know how to talk to our guys in trouble. Everybody's real happy with your work." And he waits for the other union heads to willingly or otherwise make encouraging noises.

But the guy winds up anyway and tells me in no uncertain terms about a NYPD cop being about as manly as any guy can be, and that you lose the trust of a man if you sell him out to his wife. At this the other guys start to smile and nod, a few even applaud. Now the monsignor has his head down with his hands folded in front of his face, his lip against his rings, and he gives me this baleful I-told-you-so look. So I start to fume. And I don't know what to do with it because I promised my Higher Power back in Hazelden that I'd put the anger down. But this wasn't anger like the temper I went out to fix. This was a different anger. This was like the anger my old man had running through his body when he saw Pete Cowboy push his kid against a wall and steal his box of empty bottles, when he ran the punk into a corner and punched his lights out. He didn't care if he was a big shot or not. He didn't care who he was.

"Excuse me, gentleman!" I say, and I stand up. I look over at the monsignor, and he shoots me a look and gives this little shake of the head as if to say, "Don't do it, Jim."

But it's too late. The pitch is over the plate, I'm in motion, and the words are rolling out. I've cleaned up my speech as best I can, and watch out when I clean up.

"Gentlemen!" I say again, because these guys are talking excitedly among themselves. "Excuse me! But can I say something here? Thank you. Thank you very, very much."

I walk from the table and I walk back. I didn't plan it, God knows, but I wanted their full attention and I needed to get my head together. So here I am staring at them all in the face, even Monsignor Dunne, who is glaring at me like I'm the cat that ate the canary. Then I say something like this:

"Now, I understand you represent the cops on the streets of the five boroughs of New York. I get that loud and clear. But could you please tell me this: Who is it that represents the wives of these cops who don't leave the house without sunglasses on to hide the black eyes they've got—and not one, no, both of their eyes—black as midnight. Who represents them? Could you please tell me that?" Now there's this rumble that runs through them like when you get in a good first punch and the guy falls back to get himself together. But you can't let him regroup. You have to follow up, and fast.

"And while you're at it, tell me who represents the kids locked in their rooms, pissing in their PJs with fear, waiting for their old man to kick down the door and do God-only-knows-what to their own flesh and blood because this job they got makes good men go crazy so the rest of us can walk around more or less sane. Who represents those kids? The ones who forge a driver's license to join the service at sixteen and get their faces blown off overseas before they're eighteen years of age, or run away from home to do God only knows what to eat—because they can't sleep in the house they grew up in because their father is the devil himself when he's drunk? Who represents those kids? Tell me that, would you please? Who represents them, gentlemen? And last but not least, who represents the cop's mother getting the call in the middle of the night from her daughter-in-law saying she's in fear for her life—that she can't call the cops because her husband *is* a cop, but she's in fear for her life and for the lives of her family. And to please, get over here! 'Please, I'm begging you, Ma,' she says. So you tell me this! Who represents that poor woman, torn between the son she loves and the animal he becomes when he's in a blackout? A creature threatening to kill her grandchildren and her grandchildren's mother—a woman who happens to be his wife. Who in God's name represents her or any of them? I'll tell you who! Nobody, that's who!"

Now I have their attention. It took a stick of dynamite, but I have it.

"Now you don't know me so well, but maybe you've heard I've been around, and that's the truth. Sure, I've been to some places I never want to see again. But one place I've never been is where I'm woken up in a jail cell to be told I killed somebody from my own family. And now I'm telling you something—I can stop that from happening." And I let that sink in a second. "Not every time. I wish to hell I could, but I can't. I'm just one guy. But I promise you, I can bring the numbers down. I can bring them down! I know I can! So I'm asking you, as the friends of these guys you represent, the cops of the five boroughs of New York, please, give me the tools to do my job. Because if you do, I promise you I will lower the numbers of murders within the police and police families, and the suicides and the other atrocities. If you let me bring the families in on this—because it won't work without them—if you let me have the families, I promise you I will make a change you can be proud of. Together, we will bring the numbers down. I swear to God, we will! Now excuse me, but I need some air."

And I turned and walked as fast as I could towards the door when I heard, "Cusack!"

It was like the voice of God Himself. But I knew it wasn't God; I knew it was just one of the sad, sorry human beings down here on this mixed-up world of His. So I wipe my eyes and turn around to face the owner of that voice of judgment, and I see it was the guy who gave me the hard time to begin with. He was of Irish descent, which is where he got that voice of his—back in the old country—and he was standing now, ready to let me have it but good. So he's looking over the bunch of union guys who were all there, mumbling. I couldn't see them very well because I was nearly to the door. Then I finally got up the courage to look over at Monsignor Dunne. He was pressing his lips to his rings, and I figured I'd really done it this time. So I walk back, and as I do, I get a little closer look at the monsignor, and I see his eyes are filled with tears. And I look down the line at them, and they've all got tears in their eyes, these tough union guys. So now the big shot who let me have it uses a handkerchief and then puts it back in his pocket and puts out his hand. At this point you could have blown me over with a feather. So I take his hand, and he says, "We'll bring up the families, Jim. You just tell us how you want it done." And then they all stand up because they each want to shake my hand. And at that moment, I can tell you this, on his throne down in hell, the devil himself was none too happy. And Monsignor Dunne, he knows it too. Which is why he's on his feet waiting to shake my hand while smiling to beat the band.

SEVEN

Turning the Corner

WHEN THE UNIONS for the NYPD gave me the green light to start bringing up the wives and children of these cops in trouble, it was like we turned the corner. For a minute there I was pretty nervous because I'd given it the big sell, no doubt about that. So it was my reputation at stake, too. And make no mistake, there was a learning curve for me as well. I'd explored highly successful family therapy, but there was a lot more for me to learn.

For instance, I soon had a couple in a therapy session on a sunny summer day, so warm, in fact, I'd thrown open a window. After the session this husband and wife agreed they'd opened up to each other, and that we'd made some real progress. So they were walking outside afterwards when through the open window I hear her screaming, "Son of a bitch!" So I hurry outside and ask if everything's okay. And she says, "What do you want now?" So I said I overheard her insulting her husband after I thought we'd kind of buried the hatchet and I was concerned. "My husband?" the woman shouts, getting in my face. "I wasn't calling my husband a son of a bitch. I was talking about you."

That gives you an idea maybe of some of the work I needed to attend to along the way. But the overall news was hopeful and word on the street was we were making real progress with the NYPD's drinking and related problems. Monsignor Dunne was so pleased he decided to host an event "up at The Farm." This would be a special picnic for the guys in recovery and their families which became a very special day. Fact is, there was a lot of real healing going on, everyday miracles left and right, after crawling through a tunnel of darkness a couple of thousand miles long.

Not long after this first sober NYPD picnic I got a call from my past. No one in this world has a voice quite like Mickey Diamond, smoked sandpaper with Caro syrup dribbled over it.

"Mickey!" I yell into the phone, instantly brought back to the street, "How the hell are you doing?"

"Better than ever, Jim. First time in my life I got a steady paycheck. Don't have to worry about paying the bills. It's an automatic! The sanitation union—God bless 'em—comes along and makes me king of the drunks. The sober ones, anyway. So I think you and me, Jim, we're gonna do some business like we used to in the back of the candy store, remember! But multiply that by—whooo, boy—now these sanitation men know how to drink, Cusack!"

So we brought up the sanitation workers next, and after that it was the steamfitters union, then we bring in Con Ed—and they're smart. Ahead of the game. And somewhere in the middle of this macho avalanche of alcoholic tough guys, we come to an agreement with the union heads of the FDNY—that's right, the firefighters, drinkers of legend.

It's true that when the uniformed agencies first began to work with us at Glen Acre Lodge it was all a large experiment—but we got results, so it soon became clear that recovery would need to be built into union and insurance company policies. The result was EAP, or the Employee Assistance Program. Prior to that, different agencies had different protocols: A guy in one uniform who needed rehab with us would get "docked" a certain amount from their paycheck once they were back on the job, but their families (by which I mean their wives) would continue to get that all-important check, and life went on. A guy wearing a different uniform would be loaned monies from a fund put together by the union, which he would pay back. These were almost identical, but some clients used very different strategies. Some insurance companies offered very limited health care, but it wasn't until the 1980s that across-the-board coverage included a certain amount for rehab. By then the sanitation union had run a survey on fifty alcoholic workers in recovery over two years, and found that sobered-up workers saved the company over $200,000 in sick days and injury costs alone.

But let's not get ahead too quickly. At this point, we're well into the 1960s, which as you know is maybe the craziest period in American history. Young people are rebelling from their "square" parents. Many are rejecting alcohol and picking up pot, LSD, even the opiates. Others didn't reject booze; they simply threw this new stuff on top of alcohol for a life lived almost constantly out of control. This helped spawn a youth culture which seemed to think it was one of the inalienable rights of man to stay stoned twenty-four hours a day. But this is where I fit right in—because I grew up thinking the exact same thing. I didn't do drugs because they weren't available to me, but basically, I've yet to meet an alcoholic or an addict I couldn't relate to on one level or another. And I'm not talking about liking the same ice cream! Although that stuff can get to be a habit, too. In the rooms they say if you have an addictive personality, one of four things will eventually happen to you: You can go to jail, you can go insane and get put away, you can end up dead, or you can find a Higher Power and get help. These days there's a fifth option: You can go on meds. Now, maybe that sounds a little bleak, but when you've been around a while you find it's not particularly bleak, it's particularly accurate. In the sixties and the decades following, so many people got so wasted so often for so long that it mandated a marine corps of people like myself and Mickey Diamond and the Butlers and the Carons to fight back. Call it a counterrevolution to the "turn on, tune in, and drop out" attitude. Folks like us made no bones about the fact that if you chase a buzz, if that's the way you tick, you're going to have to face that about yourself—and get help. That or face the other options I listed back a few lines. Things happened fast in the sixties. A lot of walls were torn down. Some good walls, some bad walls.

In May of 1969 we get a call from Freeport Hospital in Long Island, N. Y., asking if we have a bed for a woman named Joan. She's a dentist's wife, mother of six, whose been bouncing in and out of detox, trying meetings, then back to drinking, then back to detox, then back to meetings—around and around. So we make arrangements, and Joan comes up as a client. Then a week later Freeport calls back. Joan had made friends with Sue. Do we have another bed? So I check with Jo Spencer, "wonder woman" of the women's wing, and that all works, so we bring in a second client.

Both women were suffering withdrawal from Valium as well as alcohol. At that time Valium was not considered addictive by the American Medical Association. In treating these two young women, I now witnessed firsthand the double-headed demon of cross-addiction to prescription drugs and alcohol. Sue moves back with her mom, becomes active in her Twelve-Step Program, starts on the fast track writing for an ad company on Fifth Avenue. I'm proud of her, happy for her, and very pleased to hear her come up every three or four months to share her "experience, strength, and hope."

Then in February of 1970, my father dies. Then a year later Sue's brother Jimmy was killed by a drunk driver. Sue comes up shaken, looking for "the bedrock" of Glen Acre where she got her first real sobriety. She shares in a couple of meetings about the way it is out there. "It's not always easy. So find your sponsor. And work the steps like your life depends on them—because it does." And now, slowly, I encounter a new challenge on my journey. I find myself staring at her. Soon I'm looking for an excuse *not* to sit and talk, because it becomes problematic for me. That's all, just more . . . difficult.

Sue returns to her world. She and her mother take a trip to California, still grieving for her brother. Now what's a sober alcoholic in trouble do? "Call your sponsor!" That was ingrained in me from the start. So when I get home, I call up Joe. He's long retired from window washing by now, living on a pension with his wife. His sons are grown. In fact, he'd confided in me a few years back that one of them had the family disease. That's AA code for alcoholism. I'm on my office line and it's a weeknight, and I try to make it sound like I called for old times' sake. Joe sounds a little tired and there's that smoker's cough of his, but he plays along as he always did.

So, I'm telling him about the trip to Mexico and all when, as always, the old sorcerer cuts to the chase. "So what's eating you, Jim? Come on, you can't fool me. Never could, never will. What's on your mind, Cusack? That's why you made this call in the first place, isn't it? So let's have it. Spill!"

I admitted that he was probably right. "Yeah. I've got something eating me up pretty good," I said. "A new problem! How do you like that, Joe?"

"Well, put it on the table. Out with it," he says. "'You're only as sick as your secrets.'"

So I repeat that last one out loud to get my courage up. And then I tell him. "Well, the truth is, Joe, over the last few years—maybe I've mentioned this?—I've actually developed a real friendship with a woman." I think I hear him mumble, "Always dangerous," but I don't pay any attention and continue. "She was a client up here a couple of years ago. Then she gets her head on straight, goes out into the world, and starts making a name for herself on Fifth Avenue. Goes to meetings regularly, comes up here every three or four months to share at a women's meeting or two. Everything's upright. I mean, maybe I get a twinge every once in a while, the way you will looking at a beautiful young girl."

"Beautiful young girl," Joe coughs with his laugh. "Now you're getting down to it. All right, Shakespeare—out with it!"

"Well, I lost my dad, and she calls me up when she hears, and we have a conversation that's not just sweet—but real, you know. From the heart."

"Here we go."

"Then a year later she loses her brother who believed in her—helped her get sober, really her best friend, and so . . ."

"So?"

"She comes up to the Lodge—the place she got sober for real—and she shares in the women's meeting . . . I wasn't there, of course, but they're all in tears, I'm told. And she tells these ladies to work the steps like their lives depended on it. And it's not all rainbows and flowers on the outside. Life keeps coming at you—and death too. So get a sponsor who knows what makes you tick and trust them, and do the steps—as many as you can, until they're done. And get your life back! So this young woman becomes real suddenly, three-dimensional, and . . ."

"And? And what? Do I have to say it for you, Cusack?"

"And . . . I fall for her."

"I guessed that much. So is there something else I should know?"

"No. I've been a total professional, I mean, she doesn't have any idea, nobody does. But—well, I took this trip to Mexico with Doris and the kids to—you know, get her out of my head, but she was right there in front of me the whole time. Couldn't shake her. Fact is, yeah—I've fallen for her, Joe. Hard."

"Bound to happen! Occupational hazard and all. Well, first of all, thanks for trusting me with this, Jim. And secondly, stay the hell away from her!"

He had me laughing again, like he always did. So I loosened up and we talked for some time. Then finally he says, "Well, what's this trouble's name, Jimmy? What do we call her?

"Her name's Sue."

"Well, I've known you long enough—and we've been through a lot, so I'm just going to say it. You're in this spot because your marriage isn't a real partnership."

"I'm not arguing with you, Joe. But what do I do?"

"How much younger is this Sue than you, anyway?"

"Eleven, maybe twelve years."

"Which makes her about twenty-seven, twenty-eight?"

"About that, yeah."

"You just said my marriage wasn't a real partnership!"

"I'm a sober drunk, not a psychiatrist!"

So we laughed hard at that and then Joe started to cough like crazy.

"You okay, Joe?"

"I'm okay. You okay?"

"Not really, but I won't drink over it."

"That's all I need to hear. You can't drink over it—no matter what, right?"

"I'm right there with you on that one, pal."

"Give me a call next week, Jim. Stay in touch, work your program, be careful. And God bless."

So I went to back to work with a vengeance, fighting a war over the hearts, minds, and livers of men and women. That's a tall order, all right. It's work you can lose yourself in, and I did. But it just wasn't in the cards that I could get Sue out of my life. It's a couple of months later—maybe I'm just getting back on the beam—when she calls up and says, "Jim, you've got to help me. My sister has a real drinking problem. She's finally come to admit she's powerless over alcohol. She wants me to take her to a hotel room for a week and stay with her and not let her drink. It's crazy!"

"Bring her here," I said. "And by the way, with whom am I having the pleasure of speaking?"

So in the midst of yet another drunken drama we're laughing, this amazing young woman and me, and it all comes crashing back, the whole thing. I think maybe that's when I just kind of surrendered to it.

Sure enough, Sue brings up her sister Joan who wants a two-week crash course and doesn't see any reason it should take any longer. So I do the intake myself, and we get her situated, and you'll never guess who shows up to visit big sis in rehab. Joe comes up to see me, in fact. I guess he realizes this thing with Sue is really taking a toll and—well, the guy manages to be here when she's here, and he just so happens to have a cup of coffee with her.

"She thinks the world of you, Jim. I'll tell you that."

"She does? Really? So, what did you say to her?"

"I said you had to be careful of friendships between men and women, that you could start with an upstanding friendship and all, and then before you know it, the wind changes, things swing around, and it can get dangerous."

"And what did she say to that?"

"She sort of laughed and I thought I saw a little gleam in her eye. And then she said, 'Oh, that would never happen with Jim. He's such a gentleman.'"

"And what did you say?"

"I said, 'Nice weather we're having these days.'"

We busted a gut on that one, and then Joe started to cough something fierce, so he lit a cigarette to calm the cough down. And I said he needed to check that cough out and quit smoking.

"Quit yourself!" he answered.

Less than a month later Joe called and said he'd checked on that cough like I told him to—and the good news was that he hadn't smoked a cigarette in over a week.

"Yeah, that's good, Joe. Now what's the bad news?"

"The bad news is that there's only one thing in this world that could ever convince me to quit smoking . . . and maybe you can guess what that is."

"Lung cancer," I said.

And Joe said, "Bingo."

⁂

They call the Twelve Steps "a simple program for complicated people." Overall, I've found this to be true, but there was one "simple" idea which took a long time for me to wrap my head around, this being that a sober alcoholic must "learn to live life on life's terms." Now I would finally come to understand this was the program's polite way of admitting that terrible things happen to you in this world—sometimes several at once—and you have to stay sober anyway. Right now two of them were staring me in the face. I had both the guilt of being in love with Sue and a death warrant on Joe, and no, that wasn't a problem I could discuss with my sponsor! But my head was like a pressurized tank and I knew I had to get the pressure down somehow, so I shared what I could with program pals, about Joe's cancer.

Usually people don't like to tell folks they're dying because most human beings are terrified of death. They pull away and disappear. I didn't do that with Joe Lemon. Joe and me, we'd shared the big stuff for twenty years, so I wasn't going to back away from him now. You see, one of the amazing things about a group of alcoholics meeting in the same room at the same time for years is we talk about life and death and loneliness and pain and envy and fear and sorrow—and yes, joy, and the little pleasures that pop up like corks on water. We don't talk much about the ball game or the weather or the new restaurant in town. We can do all that after the meeting. Inside, we talk about stuff most people keep inside. Why? Because over the years we've discovered alcoholics can't stay bottled up without resorting to the bottle and losing their chance to die sober. That's a code in AA: When you hear it said that so-and-so died sober, it means they went out as an undefeated champion. Sounds easy enough, right? You've been without a drink for twenty, thirty, forty or more years? What's so tough about dying without a drink? To which I can only say—try it sometime . . . and may you be so lucky.

And the other problem? I went a different way with that.

Listening to the time bomb I had these days where my heart used to be tick, tick, ticking away, I realized I needed to surgically remove Sue from my life. But I couldn't let her go without telling her how I felt. It just seemed like a cowardly thing to do. Besides, it wouldn't work unless I told her—because she liked me. As far as she knew, I was one of the good guys, so unless I set her straight, she wouldn't know why she needed to disappear—and fast!—if I was ever going to feel anything like serenity again. But I figured, Sue's smart. She'll get it. Guys have been falling out of trees for her since forever already. I was just another old sap. But before she disappears from my life, she deserves to know why.

Every October in New York, Alcoholics Anonymous throws a big dance at the Hilton Hotel. It's that rare occasion when sober alcoholics get dressed up and go someplace fancy, where the waitress isn't pressuring you about cocktails and wine with dinner. I'd been bringing guys down there as a chaperone for years. So here we were at the Hilton, a bunch of sober alcoholics, dressed to the nines, when in walks Sue.

After we said hello, I asked, "Can we go for a cup of coffee?" So we went downstairs, got a couple of coffees, and sat alone at a table. I think she lit a cigarette. People were mulling around, but it was private enough, and I finally said, "Sue, you'd do me a favor, right? If I asked you?"

"Of course, Jim," she answered, looking a little concerned. "Anything!"

So I took a deep breath and laid it out, "If I told you that I had feelings for you that weren't proper for a married guy . . . I mean, to have such feelings for a beautiful girl more than ten years younger than me . . . if I told you that and then explained that no matter how much I valued our friendship, that these other feelings had kind of taken over and . . . Listen, I tried to get it together in Mexico, but I couldn't get you out of my mind. I'm telling you I've tried every which way to get back to just being friends, but it can't go back. So I'm going to have to ask you to stay away from the Lodge from here on out, and it's best that we kind of leave each other alone. And I'm sorry. I'm really sorry to have to say this but . . ."

Maybe I'd looked away a second or two, to help get it out. Anyway, when I looked back I saw there were tears in her eyes, which stopped me like stepping into a parked truck.

"Jim, I completely and totally understand." Sue said, looking so sad and beautiful, but with this wry little smile, too. "And I—well, you're absolutely right. I should stay away from the Lodge and get on with my life without you and our wonderful friendship because, well, the truth is, by now, I have the same kind of feelings for you."

And at that I about fell out of my chair.

———⊶⊷———

Poor Joe Lemon was getting ready to meet his maker, and here I was begging for advice like a lovesick kid.

"I'm outta my league on this one, Jimmy. What do I know 'bout this stuff? Whatever you do, I'm behind you. Hundred percent. You got that?'

"I got it, Joe. Thanks."

A week later I get a call from Joe's wife. I'm bracing myself for the worst, but she says, "Joe's right here, Jim, and he wants to talk to you, okay? But don't talk long. He's going in for an operation tomorrow and he needs all his strength."

Now Joe gets on the phone and he sounds pretty awful, all right. "Hey Jim, how are you doing?" he says. "Yeah, I got a procedure tomorrow—what're you gonna do? I'll be all right. You bet. But, Jim, this is a crazy world we're in, and so I have to ask you to promise me one thing."

"Sure, Joe," I said, "anything."

"No matter what happens, Jim—you can't drink over it. No matter what."

Well, this was nothing new. But he said it like it was something new, and that threw me for a loop. Still I knew he'd asked for an assurance from me before going under the knife, so I promised him. Sure enough, he died on the operating table the next day, and maybe the death of my father the year before and Joe's death all rolled together in my mind because . . . well, it rocked me right down to my toes. And while I was mourning the best friend I'd ever had in this world, that thing he asked me to promise him really started working on me. Ever the alcoholic, I thought there was something I'd done that Joe was especially worried about, and of course, I figured it was probably this confusion around Sue.

At the wake I took his widow aside. I apologized for interfering in her grief, but I told her I was confused about what Joe had said to me the day before he died. It was quite a scene there. The one son was an alcoholic doing what alcoholics do, the other sober and strong. Several grandchildren were sobbing the loudest. Joe's widow's tears flowed without shame, and she reached up and kissed my cheek and whispered, "He was having a hard time staying sober at the end, Jimmy. Don't you see? My Joe was talking to himself as much as he was talking to you. Do you understand now, Jim?"

I have to say that hit me like a ton of bricks. I'd never even considered the fact that Joe himself could get pulled back towards a drink. Somehow he seemed superhuman in that one way. But the truth is, he was an alcoholic, just like me, and scared to death of Death, and what does an alcoholic think of first when he's scared to death?

Well, I quit smoking around then. For good. I can't say I didn't call Sue once in a while, and write her letters about how we were doing the right thing in not seeing each other. And don't forget I was running one busy rehab, boy, oh boy, was I. But we both felt pretty awful about the whole thing, on the one hand, while on the other hand, we couldn't quite cut off all communication, either.

Sue was making preparations to move to California because— hard as it was to figure what she saw in me—I guess she felt better about relocating and starting afresh. First she went to a Catholic priest in Far Rockaway and spoke to the father about me and California, and all. Then he surprised the daylights out of her by saying he wasn't sure moving to the West Coast was the thing to do. He thought that maybe she should stay put and see this through. That if being totally sober had become part of her life's work, as it obviously had with mine, and that if we'd discovered a real, true, lasting love cementing this work, "God's wonders to perform," that it might just be the Almighty's will for us to be together. Now, when I heard this—I know this sounds crazy—but I became convinced this priest was making a play for her. Such things have happened before, believe you me! So I found an excuse to drive down to the island and pay the good father a visit. And I didn't bring flowers, follow? I didn't blow my top, mind you—and a good thing too because three minutes into the conversation, I realize this priest was totally on the up-and-up, and I was one crazy jealous jerk. In fact, talking with him really helped. I confessed I missed taking Communion, and the father said that was between God and me, and no one else could judge how I should play it. When we were finished I thanked him, and while kneeling and crossing myself properly before leaving, it became pretty clear there weren't going to be any easy answers here.

A little before Christmas I called Sue and asked if she and her mom could come up and go out for a bite. Total hypocrite! I couldn't stop seeing her, quite. If she had been shocked by my confession, it would have been different. For pride's sake, I'd have cut the cord. But knowing that she loved me too? Suddenly, this tough Irishman rolled over with all four paws in the air. I was trying to do the right thing, okay—I was. But it was getting harder and harder to do.

With Sue back in the church at this point, and what with me meeting her mother now, not as a counselor, but as a . . . whatever the hell I was! Well, the three of us spoke about the church a lot and what God's plan might be. During one hilarious conversation, Sue's mom admitted that she'd been pouring holy water into Sue's scotch for years, trying to sober her up and send her back to church with the very same potion.

But above and beyond the enjoyment of the connection it was clear Sue was highly distraught over the idea of breaking up a marriage and a family. Her mom thought if we put our relationship with God first that the rest would follow, and so, during the holiday season of 1971 I attended a Catholic Mass with them and took the holy Eucharist for the first time in many years.

This awful in-between period didn't end for months and months. Finally, I visited the sister I never had, Elaine, my sister-in-law who had saved my derriére to begin with, and she said I had to follow my heart. So that's what I did. Or that's what *we* did. It was May of 1972.

Telling Doris was bad. So yes, that was a mess. I felt pretty confident that after all I'd done for Monsignor Dunne and the NYPD there would be a job, or at least a strong recommendation for one, waiting in the city. Sue had a fantastic job as the first woman advertising manager at a Fifth Avenue firm. I figured I'd get a recovery job in one of the boroughs and return to my roots. So I signed my half of the Lodge back to Doris, packed as much of my life as I could fit into the back of my red station wagon, and drove away from that detox I'd brought back from the brink and turned into a successful business. I just left it behind, along with a marriage which had known its ups and downs—like most—the remnants of which not so many years later I would reconnect to as a stepfather and friend. Just drove away. Painful? You bet. Especially when Monsignor Dunne told me I'd abandoned the cops who'd come to trust me and a wife who gave me my start in life, "all she had and more." A job with the NYPD? Not on your life. Pay for the consequences of your actions was more like it.

So I had to punt. Sue was living with her mother while I lived on some savings and moved back in with my brother and Elaine. I went to the gym a lot to keep my head together. We were both practicing Catholics again, and we respected the laws of the Church, which meant I needed a divorce and Sue and I needed to get married—but fast. We were both getting our fair share of hairy eyeballs at meetings we attended pretty religiously.

Friends from these meetings were worried that the stresses of our dramatically changed lives put both our sobrieties at risk. And they were right, no doubt about it. But sometimes people can also be a little jealous of folks who risk it all for love, and bottom line, that's what we were doing. It was my brother, Jack, who suggested I could get a divorce and we could get married in Haiti.

And there was one plan which came together beautifully. We flew down with Sue's mother and her sober sister, Joan. The bridal suite was a gorgeous room with a view of the bay. In seven days, it was done. At the wedding celebration Sue's mother got high on champagne and told her daughter she was welcome home if it didn't work out. Even the priest back in New York had to admit our marriage was totally legal and legit in the eyes of the Church, though he added, "I'm just glad you didn't ask me about it beforehand."

Now came another difficult decision. After casting around I found all my old contacts in recovery had pulled up the drawbridge. Seems like after my departure, the program at Glen Acre Lodge wasn't experiencing the same results, and Monsignor Dunne blamed me for the increase in relapses. I had a problem with this assessment because I'd asked for a job with the NYPD which would have strengthened their program once cops returned to work, but I'd been turned down. As far as I was concerned, these unfortunate results were not in the least my fault, but I was blackballed anyway. So I faced the reality of the situation and took a job selling Equitable life insurance. I maintained strong contacts just about everywhere in the greater NYC area, and consequently, I did well and made plenty of money. But in my heart, I felt representing a different kind of life insurance was my destiny in life, and that had to do with fighting the demon of addiction. But for the moment anyway, that was behind me. I'd found the love of my life at the very instant my mission in life vanished. Still, I did my best to put a brave face on it while finding a new life with a beautiful bride on my arm, both of us stone-cold sober.

EIGHT

Back to My Mission

THE DOMINICAN SISTERS of Amityville, New York, had
maintained a huge monastic estate of 1,500 acres since
early in the last century. It included large buildings and camps,
including Saint Joseph's, a facility on over 150 acres devoted to
the recovery of tuberculosis patients and other troubled souls.
Then, with TB under control during the prosperity of the
postwar years, the estate fell on hard times. Around 1970, four
nuns were sent to Saint Joseph's from Long Island to drum up
enough income for the Dominicans to hold onto the sprawling
compound. Two of the sisters encountered a woman whose
alcoholism had been arrested by our Twelve-Step Program,
and so the idea of an alcohol treatment facility at Saint Joseph's
evolved. Soon the sisters encountered the rough but deeply
caring world of our program and were astounded by it. Through
the recovery grapevine they contacted Monsignor Dunne who,
circa 1971, carried their phone number with him to a certain
meeting of counselors in NYC.

Though I was doing well in the insurance business, Sue
encouraged me to maintain these more important contacts
and wait out the storm surrounding my leaving Glen Acre.
Unbeknownst to me, Sue's mom—who could never be called
shy—sits down a few months after we're married and writes a
letter to Monsignor Dunne. I can't tell you how polite she was
because I never saw the letter, but you can bet I was told plenty
about it later. In it she asks why, exactly, had the monsignor,
this Godly man, hardened his heart against "my son-in-law,
Jim Cusack?" What had he done that was so evil, she wanted

to know? Granted, hard as he tried not to, Jim fell in love. And
yes, he struggled bravely for many months against this passion,
as did the young woman in question. Separately and together,
this recovering young alcoholic and Jim Cusack returned to
the Holy Mother Church for guidance. They never carried
on an adulterous affair. They were told they had to be true to
themselves and to God, and that if this were the first real love
of their lives (which to the bottom of our feet, we both knew it
was), well, then they needed to be courageous and act. First, Jim
had to get a divorce (I hadn't been married in the Catholic faith,
so Monsignor Dunne would agree this was more an annulment
than a divorce), and then once Jim was free, Sue and Jim needed
to get married, a proper wedding in the Catholic Church, which
indeed had been accomplished a few months earlier on the
island of Haiti. My mother-in-law apparently laid it on thick.
God bless my mother-in-law! Somehow, she asked Monsignor
Dunne if anybody else ever had the success with the men in
blue that I had. And we all knew the answer to that question
was no. And then she tied it up with a bow, telling him that the
one sure way to give these alcoholics the chance they deserved
was to revoke the ban he, Dunne, had placed on me.

But I didn't know any of this yet. So imagine my surprise
when I bump into Dunne at this counselors' meeting and, rather
than him giving me the cold shoulder as he has in the past, he
puts out his hand, pulls me aside, and gives me a phone number,
saying I should use his name when calling these nuns so "the
prodigal son might drag his sorry self home, at last." I didn't
know what to make of it, that's for sure. But I thanked him,
sat through the meeting, and then hurried back to our place
on Long Island, bringing Sue the news. It wasn't long before
her mother told us about her letter. Then I called the nuns and
we hit it off, each speaker covering the phone and saying to

their trusted companion, "They've been waiting to hear from us!" As quickly as it could be arranged, I made an appointment and drove over to see Saint Joseph's. Well, it was overgrown and needed some sprucing up, but I didn't see it how it was; I saw it the way it soon would be, which made it the most beautiful building I'd ever set eyes on. I think Sue, on the other hand, was secretly horrified when she saw it, I guess because she'd never seen me start from scratch before.

Now began the seesaw support system of a great marriage. When I was low, Sue would bail the boat. And rare though it was that Sue got discouraged, I'd bail for her in those times. That's how it was then, and that's how it is today. What developed from our meetings with the nuns was this: Sue and I would quit our jobs and throw ourselves into preparations for establishing a rehab (with high hopes of the NYPD, FDNY, Sanitation, Con Ed, and the rest jumping back on board); we would receive no salary but what income was produced above what was needed to keep Saint Joseph's going. Bottom line, I would get back to what I was supposed to be doing in life, and Sue would be right there beside me.

We opened on May 30, 1973, and yes, we started slow. We developed the budget and logo for Veritas Villa in an attic at 36 Gordon Street. We were given a freezer full of food. We only had one phone. A first cousin of mine came in shaking like a leaf. Then we had a lawyer who wanted special permission to go to the race track in Monticello, so we sent him packing. Everybody gets the same treatment in my rehab, and that is an ironclad rule—twenty years before Betty Ford.

But back when we first started up, a couple of months crept by with Sue waiting for the phone to ring. My morning meeting had five people in it, and the thirty-cup coffee machine wouldn't get full use for a while yet. Then Monsignor Dunne decides the "recovering PD"—five hundred strong—should have their picnic up at Saint Joseph's. That was a sign that we were back in solid with the top brass. Whatever sins he figured we'd committed, we'd paid for. After that many of my best staff from Glen Acre Lodge came back to me, most memorably Ralph, whom you might remember as the drunken priest who became a (mostly) sober cook at Glen Acre. Sure, Uncle Ralph came back on board, and except for around Christmastime he stayed pretty dry. The irony was that, years later, after he was diagnosed with lung cancer, he never slipped again. Refusing hospital care except at the very end, Ralph preferred to stay with us. The last day of his life he told a friend praying with him, "I'm waiting for Sue and Jim." I don't know how he knew, but we were on our way. Sue and I each held him by a hand on opposite sides of the bed, praying quietly with him, when who should walk into the room but the priest who brought him to me at Glen Acre many, many years before. A tired but contented smile creased old Ralph's face, and we all knew it was full circle and time for our friend to head home. He died sober and with great dignity a few minutes later. What a beautiful Mass we held for him, burying him just down the road from Saint Joseph's.

———⊗⊗⊗———

Something needs to be said about passing out of the 1960s into the 1970s, 1980s, and beyond. At the beginning of the "flower power" heyday, the lines were firmly drawn. Alcohol was the drug of choice for uniformed public servants, whether we're talking cops, firemen, sanitation workers, or airline pilots and stewardesses; whereas "street drugs" were for musicians, long-haired young people, and maybe college professors. But come the 1970s, we had GIs coming home from tours of duty in Vietnam strung out on pot, heroin, you name it. Cocaine eventually becomes a "yuppie drug" which makes its way into very conservative circles, and when drugs get removed from civilians and placed in the hands of cops who happen to be human beings . . . stuff happens. It's not so black and white anymore. In the case of that uniformed public servant coming in for treatment for drugs, a case where if language to this effect appears on his file it means the end of a career? So? Here is one place I bend the rules a little so this public servant can get some help.

Narcotics Anonymous—an adaption of AA—was actually formed in the San Jose, California, area way back in 1953, but didn't find its way into prominence here on the East Coast until the 1980s. There's no way a cop can attend an NA meeting. So for the uniformed guys in recovery, we used the Twelve-Step model, and then in private meetings I just tell them to substitute their drug of choice in place of the word "alcohol." The whole thing was kept low-key. And for a while, that worked well. Monsignor had jumped in with both feet again, bless him. He came up for the holidays and would sing, very tongue-in-cheek, "I'll Be Home for Christmas"—you know, ribbing these poor guys big time. "I'll be home for Christmas—if only in my dreams." Ouch!

Due to the huge size of the place and our inclination to collect sober alcoholics and addicts the way other people collect dogs and cats, well . . . we do just that at Saint Joseph's. Folks come into the fellowship, find a Higher Power, get their addictions under control. They feel safe and loved—sometimes for the first time in their lives. They don't want to leave. We have a huge place, tons of deferred maintenance to attend to, and more beds than a comb has teeth. So they stay. Some pay, some work, some do a little of both, and some, well, for once in their lives, they get a lucky break and come along for the ride.

Before you know it we're back in the good graces of the unions and growing by leaps and bounds. Eventually, Sue and I send letters to both Millie and Doris to share our success, both financial and otherwise, with them. The response is heartfelt and welcoming, so there's healing happening in our lives. Also, since I'm being called on the carpet to speak before nuns and heads of the Dominican order, I invest in a public-speaking course offered by Dale Carnegie's outfit. To shake some of the street out of the tread in my shoes, you might say. I still use some pretty rough language (and am the only person on the team allowed to do so) when dealing with rough customers. The rehab I run is inexpensive and has an impressive track record. We cater to a blue-collar clientele, but we have no problem offering our services to the well-to-do when they've failed elsewhere, just as long as they realize they're not going to get any special treatment here. Why? Because they're not. That's why. And it's a good thing I haven't forgotten how to get tough because in the late 1970s, the newly renamed Veritas Villa at Saint Joseph's became the first free-standing rehab in New York State *not* to distinguish between drug and alcohol addictions. And—oh boy—now the manure hits the fan. And it was time for another showdown.

I suit up and show up for a big meeting in Manhattan at John Jay College with over a dozen of my industrial clients there in force. Here I tell them, "I've been bending the rules for you people for years now, calling a drug program an alcohol program to give your employees a shot at cleaning up their acts and getting back to benefitting society without a file that'll hurt their careers. Now I finally have a program in place which allows for this broad-base recovery I've offered your people discretely for years, and what thanks do I get? Now that it's on the up-and-up and open to anybody, you hypocrites bitch and moan. You don't want to hear the bedrock truth that a drug is a drug is a drug. That the treatment for wine is the same as the treatment for whiskey is the same for cocaine is the same for heroin. You don't want cops having to go into the same meeting with individuals who might be their enemies on the street. Who maybe they locked up the year before. To which I say? Tough luck! Addiction is an equal-opportunity destroyer that doesn't care what color your skin is or your hat is or how long your hair is. Addiction is my only enemy, and anybody who wants to get straight is welcome in my rehab. And if you have a problem with that, then go find some goofball outfit that does what you tell them to do and doesn't get the job done. You want the job done right? You know where to find me." And with that, I walked. Consequently, I lost seven large accounts. Two years later, they were all back. But whenever we're challenged by the world at large or a big internal problem, Sue clears our schedules for an afternoon, we take a drive up to Auriesville to the Shrine of the Martyrs, and I breath in, breath out, say prayers, ask for direction. Before you know it, I calm down, and invariably good things happen. And we return home with Auriesville holy water!

One really interesting development from a little earlier was that some of the nuns found that working with alcoholics and addicts brought them closer to their understanding of Christ's original mission. So a few of them went to school and earned degrees in recovery counseling—women who had never taken a drug in their lives! Some of them had never so much as taken a drink! And yet look—they bring some of that godly glow into a rough, tough place, and both the broken and the undefiled profit from the exchange.

I mention this now because it wasn't long before we had a real problem with the good sisters of Amityville. So I start out remembering some of the good they brought to us—and there was a lot, including (or so we thought) the fact Sue and I are assured Saint Joseph's for the rest of our natural lives so we could continue to do exactly what we were born to do. Then, in May of 1981, I was informed that the entire facility had been offered for sale without our knowledge, that a deal had been accepted, and that we had all of three months to vacate. Lock, stock, and barrel. For a minute there, thirty acres were put aside for us to build on, but that wasn't acceptable to the buyers. And don't forget, we also had thirty residents. These were the sober alcoholics who were too old to work and too broke to pay, whose families had forgotten about them, and who'd come to depend upon Sue and me as shepherds of this oddball flock. So as if it wasn't enough to have to figure out where to hang our shingle next, we had Cusack's Seniors to worry about too, about thirty-five of them.

Maybe I used up a lot of my "street tough." For whatever the reason, the news about the Villa being sold out from under us hit like a sucker punch and knocked the air out of me. It was a real shock.

Now, I know about shocks—professionally. I know what a shock can do to a sober alcoholic who thinks his troubles are over. And I'm not even talking about picking up a drink. In the rooms you hear a lot about folks who go on a "dry drunk," which means they act drunk without drinking. Well, I was pretty worked up about losing Saint Joseph's, all right. My wife, Sue, suggested I go on a retreat, what they call a cursillo. My aim was to work out the resentment I held.

When it was my turn in the all-male healing circle down at that large, log-cabin style retreat set back in the foothills of Pennsylvania, I started to open my heart up to these guys about having to pack up and leave Saint Joseph's, about the hurt and anger, and yes, the fear of what to do next, when who should walk into the room running her mouth about where my car was parked but this chalky-cheeked nun.

Maybe you've read enough of my story to guess that my mouth can run a little on the rough side. And since I'm the guy running this mouth, I think I have a pretty good idea about my swearing sessions (at least for the twenty or so years I had been sober at this point). But I have to admit, I never, ever went off on such a filthy tirade as I did while explaining that it was "a grievance against the nuns that sent me down here only to have another nun run her mouth about where I park my car." If you want to add a foul word or two before and after each of those in the sentence quoted above, you'll have it. The good news is, I was able to return home and tell my beautiful wife, "Sue, you were right as usual. I really DO feel a whole lot better. Now let's get to work!" And, oh boy, did we.

I'm not going to drag you through the wild goose chases, because there were a few of them. The best of the bunch was a guy who answered an ad we placed in a local paper. He calls up and says, "I've got just what you need—and you don't even have to buy, I'll go partners with you! The only problem—I'm being up front with you, okay?—is the place used to be a winery." Not to be accused of lacking a sense of humor, I said we'd like to see it anyway, and oddly enough, it did have everything we needed. Including enough space for Cusack's Seniors.

Even Monsignor Dunne liked it. Face it, in the old days, all the best wineries were run by monks, so these men of the cloth have a natural fondness for such. He even comes up and says a Mass to get the good vibe going. But elsewhere in the forest, the vibe is not so good. Like at the business meeting we set up before going to the local town council, where my partner says, "You take care of the alcoholics and addicts, and I'll take care of the business." That didn't sit too well. Then around the same time, a dog of his gets beaten up by neighbors to show their warm feelings about us moving forward. So we bail on the winery, and we're back to square one, and the clock isn't ticking—it's gonging!

Off to Auriesville we go for the day and pray. The next day, I answer an ad in an upstate newspaper. The real estate agent asks what exactly is it we're looking for. He's smart and to the point. When I tell him, he says, "This place you're calling about isn't what you want. I know what you want. When can you get to Kerhonkson?"

"What's in Kerhonkson?" I ask.

"Synanon is closing down its facility there. It's a perfect fit. Two separate dorms, several huge rooms for meetings, including one with a gigantic fireplace, an indoor and an outdoor pool, easy distance to the city, dirt-cheap taxes on over a hundred gorgeous acres, a motivated seller—it's all there!"

And it was all there. Finally.

Despite falling on hard times, Synanon had been founded by a recovered alcoholic, and their drug rehabilitation program was not far from the Twelve-Step model. These folks really reached out to us as brothers in recovery, and in the end, they agreed to a deal which amounted to a handshake, not a signature. I got backing from a couple of guys we sobered up. One said, "If it works out, pay me back, and if it doesn't, Jim . . . don't worry about it. What you did for me doesn't have a price tag on it."

So Sue and I emptied out our savings accounts and added these sums to the loans, finally scraping together a $100,000 down payment. Unbeknownst to our attorneys, all the retired Dominican Sisters in the Mother House in Amityville were praying daily for everyone at the Villa and especially for our mission to find a home. A Sister Polycarpa, about ninety-seven and very ill, told Sue to tell me not to worry, that everything would work out. We discovered later that day, at the exact time the two attorneys discovered a way to finalize the sale, 2:00 p.m. on October 9, 1981, Sister Polycarpa passed away. Coincidental or providential? Either way, we honor her memory, her life and loyalty, and her love of our Villa mission. Possession was granted before we actually owned the place. The technicalities included a twenty-thousand gallon of fuel oil in tanks no one knew about, and on and on. A few months later we paid what we said we would and, thanks to the good will extended to us by Synanon, we made the transition in a single day. By which I mean that someone in recovery on Tuesday in the Villa at Saint Joseph's continued on with their recovery the next day at our new location on a back country road in Kerhonkson at the new Veritas Villa. Now that's cooking with the kind of gas only supplied with a little help from above—together with a lot of holy water!

NINE

Putting Out Fires

AS YOU'VE PROBABLY NOTICED by now, veering in and out of various states of emergency is nothing new to us. Being adaptable to any and all new situations is part and parcel of running any restaurant, hotel, spa, jail, church, hospital, or detox. In fact, a detox is all those other public services rolled into one. In short, you could say what we do is put out fires without showing much in the way of panic.

Folks arriving at our door—some willing, some coerced—are in a semi-stabilized state of emergency. They're struggling to overcome a compulsion which a psychoanalyst would call a "fully manifested death wish" and defeat it with the strength of a force above and beyond themselves called a "Higher Power." The battle between these forces is nothing less than a struggle between life and death. The fact that we have a high success rate and a relatively low fee means we have a lot of traffic—call it a human highway, with entrance ramps, the main thoroughfare, and a planned exit—when a client will hopefully reenter society armed with "a program" for survival.

I'm not going to go through the entire Twelve-Step program with you as I did in another book I wrote, *Always Aware*, but I'll discuss the first three steps of AA here. I'll also explain a few key strategies which, over the years, I've used as a fire extinguisher on a flaming ego, what in our Program lingo is called "self-will run riot," which the addictive mind uses to derail the recovery process. Whether it's the cynicism I was filled with for years, or the negative ego problem of self-pity, or the arrogance of a "terminally unique" individual (one who can't possibly respond to a program which has worked for others), or any number of dodges this (creature hunted by addiction) deploys attempting to survive—I've dealt with them all.

It's like this: Addicts and alcoholics are turned over to us after being detoxed, in other words, the physical "need" to use has been defeated and will remain defeated unless and until they somehow get their hands on their drug of choice or a gateway drug that reawakens a physical craving. We say that addiction is a threefold disease that preys on body, mind, and spirit. So when an addict comes through our front doors, one of three shackles, the "body" chain, has been removed. And don't doubt it! We do have the occasional guest arrive in prison garb with chains on hands and feet, accompanied by a police officer or two who then release the prisoner to our care; this is often, but not always, a DWI offender. Result? The fully potent aspects of addiction still operative in a new client are those of the mind and spirit. Of course, agnostics or atheists might question the very existence of "spirit." I'll get to them in a minute.

As you know, we have a lot of police, firemen, sanitation workers, welders, pilots, and other pretty macho characters at the Villa. So the very first phrase of the first step of our Twelve-Step Program, namely, "we admitted we were powerless over alcohol" is an extremely difficult pill for a lot of these tough guys to swallow. Coming into the program in the postwar years after the United States of America had fronted the allied victory over forces of evil threatening the world at large, I too had no interest in considering myself "powerless." So Joe Lemon told me I was "power-*full*" when I refused to take a drink, and that I remained powerful every minute of every hour of today (which is all we have!) that I win the war against that first drink. (He had said, "It's not the caboose that kills you when you step into the path of an oncoming train, Cusack! It's the engine. Remember that when you think you could 'just have one.'") The second part of the first step is what I concentrate on with newcomers when I ask them, "Why are you here?" I'm looking for that foot in the door, that single torch on the dark hallway which is Step One. When do I get it? When I get an alcoholic to agree "that our lives had become unmanageable."

Step Two is also a minefield, especially for today's agnostic or atheist: "We came to believe that a Power greater than ourselves could restore us to sanity." Of course, you've got these guys that are too cool to go to church or synagogue or a mosque or a temple. They say, "What power is greater than me? Show it to me." But they've already stepped into an ambush, and I have them: "Your drug of choice was the power greater than yourself which you resorted to when the world got to be too much," I tell these wiseacres. "But that was a power greater than yourself which robbed you of sanity, so now you've got to switch sides in the war. You've got to find another power greater even than that dark power you worshipped. You've got to switch to one greater than that which took your sanity away in order to restore that sanity."

Once in a while I get some college-educated character who wants to go lob a grenade or two into the Twelve Steps. So I tell him to look up the letter Carl Jung wrote to Bill W. in 1961 which appears in Alcoholics Anonymous and finishes with this: "Alcohol in Latin is 'Spiritus,' and you can use the same word for the highest religious experience as well as the most depraving poison. The helpful formula therefore is: Spiritus Contra Spiritum." Or in plain English, you can only drive out the Spirit of Alcohol with the Spirit of God.

A lot of folks in recovery say if you can accept the first three steps into your life, you can stay sober; others say you can stay sober if you simply master Step One. But now in Step Three, we've got a humdinger. And here is where some tough guys start to scratch their heads and mutter under their breath about how they didn't sign on to become priests; they just want to keep their jobs, marriage, family, or sanity. To which I quote back the famous qualifier at the end of *The Big Book*, chapter 5, "How It Works": "No one among us has been able to maintain anything like perfect adherence to these principles. We are not saints. The point is that we are willing to grow along spiritual lines. The principles we have set down are guides to progress. We claim spiritual progress rather than spiritual perfection."

Step Three: "Made a decision to turn our will and our lives over to the care of God *as we understood Him.*"

You've heard of folks who have trouble believing in God—any kind of God. Okay. So their Higher Power might be their kids or their marriage or their parents; they might call "Group of Drunks," G.O.D.—that is, their meeting itself—which is a little risky, because meetings are made up of people, and people are not perfect. (Maybe you've noticed?) G.O.D. is also an acronym for "Good Orderly Direction." Using such a Higher Power consists of making a series of moral choices that do as little harm as possible. The idea is that as active alcoholics we behaved immorally and unkindly for so long that by acting fairly and with kindness we can't help but undo much harm and level the field. By "cleaning up our side of the street" we've created a place where healing can begin and real spiritual progress can take shape. Old-timers will also tell you to "act as if"—that is, pretend there is a God even if you don't believe in one. Why? Because results coming from praying to a God you are pretending exists often leads to believing in one who does! If finding a Higher Power continues to be a problem, read (or reread) "We Agnostics," chapter 4 in *Alcoholics Anonymous*, aka *The Big Book*.

What I've been sharing with you, and what you'll see for yourself if you or a loved one has cause to pay us a visit at the Villa, may seem a little counterintuitive. I'm told that when you study philosophy in school, you have to prove an argument before you put stock in it, which in our case means using logic to defend the existence of a Higher Power before we take a chance on actually using such a spiritual force to climb up and out of hell. But let's look at the dilemma head on: When you're brought here to the Villa you are not a happy camper. Your "logical mind" has failed to master the compulsion(s) of addiction. You—or at least those around you—are at the end of your rope. So what I am proposing is that you extend "the rope" with a spiritual program which may have no other proof aside from the fact that it works.

Put it this way: If I show an uneducated person how, by stroking a piece of steel with a magnet, I can also turn that piece of steel into a magnet, that person is going to say I'm a magician. Is he correct? Yes and no. What they call "miraculous" I call "science"—but the result is the same. Maybe one day they'll have enough education to understand what is happening when the steel becomes a magnet. And maybe one day we'll have evolved enough in understanding the laws of spirituality to know how and why "the miracle" of sobriety occurs. In the meantime, for those of us at the end of that rope—why don't we make sure it isn't soon tied in a hangman's knot, and leave the whys and wherefores of recovery for sometime when we aren't in such danger?

⸻

Based on our history here at the Villa we have a little better than a 70% recovery rate. But as I've said before, this does not mean we succeed every time on a first visit. So, what do I say to the returnee who "slipped" or needs a "tune-up," or "picked up," or "fell off the wagon," or "didn't get it," or "lost it?" I tell them, "What did you lose? What slipped? How did you suddenly 'not get' something you previously 'got'?" Usually they now look at me shamefaced, baffled, and otherwise confused until I tell them, "Obviously, you never really 'got it' in the first place! Maybe we tilled the field and planted a seed, but it didn't take root, it didn't grow and mature—or you wouldn't be sitting here." What's important is that a slip isn't a "slip," because if you slip, you were never on really firm ground to begin with. You never nailed Step Three, for instance. And you never forgave yourself whatever it is you're numbing yourself to when you pick up that first drink. How do I know? Because you drank! They say you never forget how to ride a bike, right? That doesn't mean you don't fall over a couple of times until you actually learn. But once you "get it" you don't forget it. Well, that's sobriety!

A lot of tough guys complain about being "mandated" to come and enjoy a month with us here at the Villa. These are the ones I promptly remind, "No one made you come here. You don't like it? Leave! No, I'll arrange a car myself. Because listen, pal, you were given a choice to go to jail or lose your job or pay us a visit. You chose to come here."

I think I demonstrated what came to be called "tough love" long before the term became popular. Breaking heads to open minds. Perhaps after all this you might appreciate why I prefer the word "evolve" to "surrender," which is a word people make a big deal of in recovery these days. "You've got to surrender to the program," they say, or "You're powerless over alcohol and you have to surrender to the Twelve Steps." But the word "surrender" itself does not appear once in the Twelve Steps of AA. And for the tough guys I have in my rehab? Just like for the World War II vets who saved the world from fascism, for them "surrendering" is the equivalent of giving up and giving in or being a coward, not being a man. That's why I prefer to use "evolve," because with "evolution" the meaning of manhood shifts, and rather than a tough guy needing to bow down in defeat, it's a different tune we sing. Around here a "real man" has guts enough to get sober, a "real man" has guts enough to make amends to his family and friends over the wrong he's done and the hurt he's caused. A "real man" walks the talk rather than talking the walk. And you know what else? A real man is capable of giving and receiving real love. That's where I lucked out!

So here we are at the heartbreak hotel where I spend my days putting out fires. That's really most of what I do and what I've been doing from the beginning. And we finally found the perfect place to do it—where the Villa was intended to be. So yes, I've gotten over my resentments concerning the sisters of Amityville and have welcomed them back into my heart. And Sue's sister, Joan, who insisted I get her sober in two weeks because she didn't have time for anything longer, remember her? Well, the joke was on us. Joan got it in those two weeks and never took another drink. In fact, she became highly involved in the Program and eventually came here for a year in 1982 and helped Sue set up our women's program. Briefly, we tried having coeducational meetings. With the low number of guests, we thought we could eliminate the courtship dance. But both men and women and their families appreciate the separation so they can focus on the challenge at hand—addiction. Unfortunately, romance is maybe "the first" addiction known to humanity.

We had a young man once who had relapsed around a break-up with his girlfriend and was brought to us in a desperate state. I ordered that he remain accompanied at all times to prevent a tragedy. His chaperone disappeared for five minutes to bring back some lunch, and in those few moments, the demon of self-destruction slipped through our defenses and invaded this struggling addict's love-obsessed mind. This young man was found hanging moments later, with pictures of his girlfriend strewn around the floor below.

What I'm saying to you is this: Compulsive attraction is a high, like a drug; it's dangerous, highly inflammatory, and at best, incredibly distracting.

Now, before I make myself out to be some modern-day Saint George slaying the dragon of addiction each and every time it so much as belches, let me rat myself out and admit sadly, it isn't so. We don't always win. Tragedies occur—as you've seen. That's simply a reality.

And personal sadnesses don't stop, either. For instance, Sue and I both lost our mothers in 1982. Sue's mom was a fireball with a wide circle of friends. She was full of life, a loving, outgoing force of good who made every day count and left a hole when she passed. My mother was a wise, quiet, prayerful old Irishwoman, still with her brogue. She showed up at the Villa one morning with a friend. They had driven through the night. We had no idea they were coming. Soon after, Ma moved up here full time to a home on the Villa grounds. As always, she spent a lot of time with the nuns and priests. One morning I had the urge to walk over early and have breakfast with her. I'm sorry to say, this wasn't a usual thing I did. We sipped on a second cup of coffee together and she said, "Oh, but you weren't *so* terrible, Jimmy. And you've made me proud—your father, too—God rest his soul."

I gave her a kiss on the top of her head and told her I loved her, and I wish that were something I said more often, but it wasn't. I went to the bank on an errand and someone said, "There's a call for you, Mr. Cusack." And I knew what the message would be. It would be Sue telling me my mother had just passed away.

When we're kids we're told that every human being is unique. That's to boost our self-esteem to make us feel like we can actually defeat the power of gravity, which says, "Why get up in the morning? It's nicer here in bed!" But no, we're unique like snowflakes—no two ever alike— we have a destiny to fulfill, so get up and fulfill it! Here at the Villa it's fine and dandy to remember that every human being is unique, but what's more important and what allows us to save tens of thousands of lives is that, while we may be unique, more importantly, we're also all the same. And you know what else is all the same? Addiction. And by the time you get here, your addiction is a demon that has been driven into a corner. It's scared, desperate, and fighting for its life—a lot like its host, by which I mean you. In this traumatized state both you and your addiction will behave in one of a few ways which—sorry to say—are anything but unique. But really, that's the good news. Because I know every step on this dance floor. I know every fire pit on the devil's picnic ground. I've dedicated my life to destroying that devil riding on your shoulder.

TEN

Bringing Our Message to the World

WITHOUT PLANNING any such ambitious efforts the Villa ended up mentoring a few international alcoholism rehabs. I doubt we were the first in this regard, but it felt that way. It all began with me teaching a course in addiction and recovery at Rutgers University. Rutgers had an exchange program with Iceland, so there was a fair amount of back and forth between the two countries, including a powerful judge who came over to visit his daughter—a recent émigré to this country. It seems on one of these visits the judge got dangerously drunk a couple of times, and his daughter, who worked at a nearby hospital well known to the Villa, was pretty familiar with our program. So she had her father detoxed at the hospital and then she sent him up here for maybe six weeks—which isn't long and isn't short, in the scheme of recovery. Lo and behold, while he was here he became what we call "a true believer." He gets the program to the bottom of his feet, and he's on what in the rooms they call "the pink cloud"—that is, a feeling of being delivered out of ignorance and misery into a state of grace. Of course, you never know what will happen out in the real world, but for a period of time anyway, he's in love with sobriety. When he leaves, he's emotionally overwhelmed by the experience and extremely grateful to us. Personally, I'm not sure what kind of a chance he really has to turn his life around because I do a little research, in fact, and I find out there's maybe one AA meeting in the whole of Iceland. So he's going to be challenged in remaining sober. Big time.

But there he is, back in Iceland, a high-powered judge head over heels for recovery. He goes straight to the top, meets with the heads of the government, tells them what we've got going here, and how it's changed his life, and what he thinks we could do for the young people of Iceland, who are—to tell you the truth—trashed. Eventually, we see pictures of drunken young men literally dragging their girlfriends by the hair over these icy sidewalks while the girls are unconscious. They wake up with a hangover and a sore scalp and think nothing of it. And yet at the same time Iceland has one of the highest literacy rates in the world, so here's this incredible potential which is—you might say—"frozen" by this ice age of alcoholism. Because it's one of these remote places on the planet where drinking is a totally accepted way of life. Imagine Ireland times five, the high and the low, everybody wasted. After a few months the heads of state reach out to us. So we negotiate a contract, and sure enough they fly a bunch of high-level heavy hitters straight onto the runway of JFK Airport—first-class passengers drinking big time the whole flight. They know it's going to be Sober City the moment they hit terra firma, so by the time they touch down they're wiped out but good. So we have them shuttled over to Freeport to be detoxed and then sent straight up here to the Villa—first-time Charlies, hit between the eyes with Step One. Then it's the whole enchilada, A to Z. They're here for about two months. But one of the conditions of the contract is they have to have a day off before flying home to go shopping. Because of the difference in prices. How many chaperones did we send along for that three-ring circus? I think three. The whole arrangement goes on for a couple of years, with a few hundred clients a year flying back home to Iceland talking about "powerlessness over alcohol" and "turning your life over to a power greater than yourself." Just think about that! Think about what sober, well-groomed

VIPS could do. They've dropped twenty, thirty pounds, and feel better than they have since they were fifteen. Besides that, they can actually remember what they said to you on the phone past 9:00 at night. We're talking about a game-changer in Iceland.

So that's one for the history books. Send them over legless and get them back in tip-top shape, mind and body. Of course, we'd had folks from Dublin and other places. But this was a government taking a long look at itself, seeing a problem, and reaching outside its own borders for help. It got to the point where the government of Iceland decided they'd do better to send us over to them to bring a sober awareness to school kids, for one. A number of our people went over: Sue and I went, one of the nuns, a few others. So we're being polite for starters and asking what they have in the way of substance abuse in junior high school, and they denied having a problem. But later, this one principal takes us back in the woods to show us a still the kids had set up for making their own hooch—the hard stuff. Forget the beer and wine of youth, straight to the knockout drops. So we get the literature translated into Icelandic, set up a number of AA meetings, then before you know it, the Icelanders take the bull by the horns and outdo their teachers. Not only did they establish detox clinics based on the Villa, but they built safe houses and halfway houses and started programs for the rehabilitation of young people. These would become recovered youths with a real shot at returning to society, with time enough to still make a contribution to society while creating healthy lives for themselves—which is, after all, what we're all working towards here, anyway.

Then we had a domino effect. Soon Denmark wanted the same thing. Over there the Danes called their first detox "The Villa," in honor of us. Soon Russian doctors and engineers were coming around, reaching out with the "new thinking" provided in Glasnost, Gorbachev being the first Soviet premiere to look their national drinking problem dead in the eye. Then, before you know it, they're bragging about a 100% recovery rate. How's that, you say? Well, let me explain. Their "program" for recovery was as follows: Encountering an alcoholic, the State would lock them up in a facility with a high barbed-wire fence around it and guard dogs stalking the perimeter. So it was sober up or else. Pretty soon I think they wised up and found that an alcoholic is an alcoholic is an alcoholic, and no matter the consequence, he or she is going back out. So soon, despite this "perfect recovery rate," they're over here investigating. One delegation visited Hazelden. I don't know if it was the same bunch or not, but we entertained a group, too. Basically, it was the same as with Iceland. They sent over these "experts," all of whom were heavy drinkers themselves. But they weren't called "alcoholics." It was like back in Ireland, where you'd never hear the word "alcoholic." Drunkenness was a socially accepted way of life; but life had changed and being drunk all the time ceased to work in what life had become.

Our Russian guests were over here for six months. We accompanied them here and there, all over, to different detox units with slightly different approaches, you might say. I guess the Villa has this boot-camp reputation because I'm from the street; yet we have a pretty high success rate and a very loyal alumni, a strong rapport with recoverees, and some high-profile supporters who say some nice things about us. And maybe I ruffle a few feathers here and there. But the Russians like us. In a way, maybe we represent what communism was supposed to be, you know—nobody better than anybody else. Not that I cop an attitude. Because I know I'm only one drink away from panhandling and waking up on a park bench.

Sure, we bonded with the Russians. And they were smart. Very. High-ranking doctors with degrees a mile long, it didn't matter. When they sensed these big shots in the fancy detox units we'd visit were giving us the cold shoulder, they'd pretend they didn't speak English. It would be Russian only. I couldn't figure it out at first, and then I realized it was their way of protesting these clowns' lack of respect for me. They'd speak only Russian, and the whole visit would come screeching to a halt. I didn't say anything, but I got the picture, and truthfully, I was touched.

We took them all over, and finally I brought them down to see the Statue of Liberty. So there we are on the ferry going out, and the seagulls are screeching, the waves are rocking and splashing the boat, the wind is blowing, and salt air is as invigorating as can be. Everybody's smiling. They're clicking pictures. Then I think I'm seeing things because these well-dressed, university-educated Russian folks—all wearing their red, white, and blue Villa jackets—are looking up at this symbol that represents their enemy's greatest PR scheme. I mean, we're all polite and I know the score about them liking me and all, but deep down, everybody knows we're still on opposing teams, until all at once, as we're approaching the landing for the Statue of Liberty, suddenly this hush comes over the deck, and I look back, and there are tears rolling down their cheeks. And I mean, to a man, every one of them is weeping. I never wept visiting the Statue of Liberty before, but that day I did.

And that's when I realized we'd gotten through to them, all right. And sure enough, they're trying to figure out how to use the program back home in the USSR. How to find a way for the State to allow the use of the word "God" when their founding father, Karl Marx, called religion "the opiate of the masses." Make no mistake, they know I'm Catholic (and sure enough, we have many a crucifix around the Villa), but they also know I'm alcoholic, and it's the "God of our understanding" that appears in AA literature, which I insist—along with "Higher Power"—be used by our counselors. Because believe you me, Bill Wilson went through hell and back to leave the word "God" open to interpretation. He even left some wiggle room for the agnostic and the atheist.

It seems Sue and I worked seven days a week back then. Coming up through the 1970s and 1980s we were this tough little engine that could, which climbed many a mountain. But some other folks had joined the field. The lonely pioneers of Twelve-Step philosophy gradually found themselves surrounded by professionals who'd figured out that there was a fortune to made in battling the demons that beset modern America—and the world. And what was the first thing they deduced about making that fortune? Can you guess?

Yes, by 1990 the "extremist" views of Twelve-Step programs had been modified. The only problem being that, as the founders of AA had predicted, "half measures availed us nothing," as one famous proponent of controlled drinking was forced to admit on television after she also admitted full responsibility in a DWI fatality. The trend in recovery was watering down the tried-and-true Twelve-Step philosophy we know works. Sue and I didn't want fads or trends burying the life-saving, soul-rescuing work we'd helped pioneer, so we began to reach out to the new generation, and to seek a powerful institution as patron to help us carry on our work.

First we went back to Hazelden. The founders had passed since I was there as a young man looking for guidance freely given and gladly received. And frankly, their approach had changed. It turned out to be more or less the same down at another foundation. We tried to link up with a powerhouse in order to safeguard this sanctuary of ours. We wanted the comfort of knowing we could put our worries to rest, assured that our work would continue on once we're gone. For a long time we were frustrated, and truthfully, for a long time Sue and I thought maybe we'd failed and let this family of ours down.

We explored a link-up with a few other places, but finding these struggling with internal problems, we pushed on.

Truth is, every place we went we found something that really troubled us. And for myself and Sue, at least, we learned that trouble is a gift. And I need to remember that. Because the moment I try to take the trouble out of it I start to get soft, and when I get soft I put my feet up and figure I can take it easy for an hour or two, maybe take the afternoon off. And soon I'm feeling like maybe I served my time—did my tour of duty—trained younger counselors to look after younger people in trouble. That maybe it's really mostly about pills these days, and what do I know about pills? But what am I really doing when I think stuff like this? I'm looking for a way out. I've lost my fire, my sense of mission.

The boardrooms and luncheons, the CEOs' offices, going out to dinner—in those places you can lose sight of the miracle which is the only reason we're doing this work in the first place. While someone is going on about "the new paradigm" and "the pharmaceutical shift," I look across the table at my beautiful bride, and I see that troubled look on her face like when we were trying to find our way through a maze of confusion, back before I had the honor of calling her my wife. And sure enough, she glances over at me and we sort of roll our eyes together and—well, it's painful, yes. Because we know it isn't going to work here with these people, either. And we feel bad about it, but it's funny too, because it's just another joke God is playing on us and all our big plans. Another test to see if we're the people we started out as or if the body snatchers have gotten us too, and we're just talking the talk and going through the motions. Forgetting to keep it green.

Finally, in 2005, we heard again from a new team heading
another treatment center—where our search had begun. But
our own process had finally come full circle and—how to put
it?—we'd actually found that *we* were what we'd been looking
for the last fifteen years. It was all here with us and had been
from the start. By then Sue and I had realized a lot of things,
among them that this book needed to be written, that we'd find
or create within our own walls whatever was needed to protect
and insure that our work would survive us, and that our message
of hope needed to be sent out into the world.

⸻⸎⸻

Early in 2007, a sign went up one hundred feet from the
main building stating that as of July 24, 2008, Veritas Villa
would comply with State of New York legislation requiring that
no tobacco products be used on the premises or carried beyond
this point. New York was the first state in the union to pass
such laws. And bingo! We had the opportunity to halt the other
major poison unleashed upon this age. So this new legislation
carries a healing message, but it also divides humanity down
the middle. Nonsmokers start to stand up and take back the
workplace. Smokers feel like they are being shoved around in
the land of the free. But here, inside a sanctuary where hurt
people come to be healed, Sue and I knew we had no choice.
We had to go to the wall on this one. But as these huge changes
were taking place, men and women all up and down this tough
world of recovery—I'm talking both guests and staff—started
to complain, big time. Any employee who couldn't or wouldn't
give up cigarettes for their working day, and that included not
coming back from lunch smelling like an ashtray, was offered
four weeks' severance pay. Two or three took us up on it; others
struggled with quitting, hoping they'd either find new strength

or that we'd get beaten up by our clients to the extent that we'd roll over. There was a huge backlash from within our own ranks because other rehabs, as well as hospitals, schools, you name it, were finding a loophole by constructing shelters for smokers to use "outside" a tobacco-free building. OASAS wasn't allowing this loophole, but neither were they cracking down as hard they might have. So we were seen as hardliners, insensitive to the spirit of compromise, and so on and so forth.

At the Villa we applaud the courage used to pass this important legislation, and we deplore the cowardice which has found the means to duck these laws. At the Villa we won't compromise the OASAS rulings. We will run a completely alcohol-free, drug-free, and yes, tobacco-free facility—without exception. So those employers who want their people to get free and live longer, healthier lives and pay them back for their generosity with longer, healthier, more productive careers, send those people to us, and we will support them while they sweat out all their demons at once. I wouldn't separate the alcoholics from the addicts because the argument for separating them was bull—and I won't go for bull because I'm not built that way.

It was a wild-card war, all right. Last thing in the world I'd foreseen happening. But sometimes you show up to fight one enemy and they've sent another one along for back up. So it becomes a war on two fronts, or if you're cross-addicted to pills and alcohol and cigarettes, it's a three-front war, and you don't have the luxury to pick the battle anymore. You're up there and you have to fight whoever is sent against you. It's where you've chosen to be, so it's nobody's fault but your own. So? We lost some clients. Some came back, some didn't. Some sent thank-yous.

It took fifteen years to realize that we hadn't failed. In fact, we had succeeded. One guy I talked to explained that what we'd experienced is called an "upwards failure." At first I thought he was crazy. Then after talking about it with Sue, we realized he was right, that the big link-up never happened because we finally realized that *we're* the ones who are supposed to do what it is we're doing to maintain our simple, pure recovery message.

——⁂——

We're a bubble here at the Villa, a sanctuary temporarily removed from the rest of the world so those who visit us can be assisted in making of themselves different men or women than the ones who walked through our doors. Maybe Sue and I are at the center of this sanctuary because we live right across the street on the grounds of the hundred-plus acre compound, and because we try to project a belief in the everyday miracle of recovery, available to anyone who works to achieve it. For the first few decades here, at what we knew would be our last home, we didn't get away much. And when we did we couldn't wait to get back, why? Because we are at our best here, and who doesn't want to do and be their best? Sue read to me one night about a wise old Greek named Socrates who believed good would always win over evil. Because, he said, in the end, doing good was more pleasurable than doing evil! I wish we had him back to lead the revolution.

In our sanctuary, guests can't use cell phones or computers. The TV is only on at certain hours—and it's not a free-for-all—not in the least. This is why the news was delayed that beautiful early fall day when a jet airliner went off course without explanation, flew into the off-limits airspace over New York City, and crashed directly into one of the World Trade Towers. Moments later a second highjacked jet struck the second tower, and within three hours both our highest buildings, spitting flame and smoke, crashed to the streets below, killing thousands of Americans—the first act of war perpetrated by an outside power against the continental United States in its history.

Now it just so happened that we had several Muslims as guests—both Arab Muslims and African American Muslims. Of course, we also had our usual clients from the police and fire departments, sanitation workers, and some hard-hat workers not known for their extremely open-minded politics. So we let the news out a little at a time, and we weren't sure where it would go. There was a lot of anger and a lot of fear, some yelling and finger pointing breaking out in the main rec room, and these weren't the kind of guys who yell to hear themselves yell.

These were more the kind of guys who let bullets fly or, failing that, used broken furniture for weapons, or—at the very least—bloodied fists at the drop of a hat. So I was down there with them in the rec room in the blink of an eye. We have quite a bit of muscle on staff, and it was down there with me.

Soon angry clients are yelling at me for not allowing the news on. "CNN! Put on CNN! This is a state of emergency! Could be a state of war!"

So I took the fire for a few minutes to get the focus onto me and away from a Muslim/Christian face-off. And then I said, "Okay, look! I agree these are not ordinary circumstances, and if we can agree to a few things, then I'll put on the news for an update. The first thing is that no matter what happens, our first priority remains unchanged—you're here to get straight and sober. Whether we have war or peace. So the TV is not going to stay on—understand? We'll get an update and then we're going to turn off the news and look at where we are in terms of our recovery. Not how we can start our own little war! Now, if we can use this crazy world as a lesson in how to do things differently—here at the Villa, right here, right now— then I'll put on CNN every couple of hours for ten minutes. If not? We're going to lock this place down—and you'll all go to your rooms until further notice. If you make trouble—I have an order for a call to go into the state police, and that's no bluff, and they're not as nice as me—as maybe some of you know! Okay? The first thing we need is a moment of silence to say a prayer to our Higher Power, and no, we don't all have the same name for this force, but I'm asking for a moment of prayer for those hurt and in danger, and for their families too."

So we had a moment of silence, and on the heels of that we watched ten minutes of news. There was a flare-up or two, but we kept coming back to looking at it from a recovery point of view. Now remember—the president of the United States was on Air Force One at an undisclosed location, we had a third jet still in the sky headed, it seemed, for the nation's capital, we had some kind of an aircraft or bomb which actually attacked the Pentagon. It felt like war, all right. But we kept it together, and then after the news, we went into the fishbowl, which is what we call the classroom of the dining common, and we approached the madness like it was something people had done in hatred, blindness, and ignorance.

I asked, "Haven't we all done stuff in hatred we later regret?"

Everyone agreed they had. And so, yes, we did some mourning, big time. We did some praying for guidance and for understanding. Christian, Jew, *and* Muslim—who were anxious for it to be known that they weren't terrorists. That they believed in America and democracy and the right to worship as they believed. All transportation had been closed down, phone lines were overloaded, and cell towers were not working in many places. Fear and panic were rampant. Our main focus that day was to keep our people here, and we did all that was possible to help them reach their families and process this horrific tragedy. That day we had people from all cultures in treatment and were able to transcend all those differences in the common bond of pain and loss. We banded together all day and night for the strength to go on, and with the power of prayer and fellowship, we realized "it is in the giving we receive," and that, yes, trouble is a gift that has made us stronger and more caring. I was very gratified with the response and caring that we all received from each other.

When we break down the walls and we become human again, this is the stuff that happens that makes life beautiful and gives us hope. This is what's supposed to happen. So before you know it these guys are hanging out together, and they've reached out to each other, and there's this bond between them. Suddenly it becomes okay for other guys in polarized situations to do the same thing, to befriend each other. Reach through the bars and find, not an enemy, but a brother in recovery. Now all at once it's like a buddy movie down there in the fishbowl. You can't make this stuff up, and it's not a coincidence either. Not that I'm preaching religion, but for every man in that room it was a spiritual experience. As if God were communicating with us through the actions of human beings.

What has emerged for Sue and me over the years of searching is that, although we had been unable to have our own child, the Villa had become our baby, and we run it like a big family, including a few spats but also a fierce joy and pride in knowing we were giving our very best. We break bread with our people at least once a week. Several local restaurants do very well hosting a large, sprawling table of folks connected to the Villa who never drink alcohol, but laugh often and eat well. In the late summer these days, Sue and I get away most weekends, but we call in regularly and find by Sunday night we miss the place and the people. When we get out locally, we always let the team know where we are, and drop-ins for dinner at this place or that are always welcome.

We have created a nonprofit foundation which makes Veritas Villa into an indestructible institution that can't be turned into a hotel or sold to a developer; it must remain what it is. In 2010, we had a meeting with all our employees and basically gave the facility to them and the future staff. Sue and I remain at the head of the board of directors, a group of accountants and attorneys who have been our loyal associates for years, and we retain our hands-on approach. We still lead the way for now, but we are turning more and more power over to our staff, and they are doing us proud. Villa Veritas will go on after us. And the hard-earned lessons of a hard-earned recovery will not be lost to troubled souls in need of exactly the treasure we have and hold—here, now, and in a future Sue and I won't ever know.

Everybody on our team has this mission. We wouldn't have people here who didn't have it. Folks who go the extra mile, who have that do-or-die thing in them, that thing that says, "I will get through to this person if it takes all night." Whatever it takes to get you through, to keep you alive to be sitting in front of me or Sue or a half-dozen people here who care about you. Until the grand slam switcheroo takes place and suddenly it's *you* who have become the person holding out the hand of hope—you! You who's got a real life and a real mission in recovery. And who are you holding your hand out to? Well, who else but another version of yourself.

I've seen myself in the eyes of those in terrible shape a thousand times. And I remember my sponsor, Joe L., the window washer from Queens who finally scraped his squeegee through the crap spattered across these peepholes of mine. And I know he's alive in me. That he's passed on the torch in the marathon of recovery. Just as maybe I pass it on today talking with you here.

And that scared, angry, desperate version of me, fidgeting in the hot seat—bringing up the poisons, sweating out the ghosts, wondering when this guy Cusack will have had enough of them and say, "We can't help you here." Have I ever said that? Not if that person in the hot seat says they'll work with me. If they'll work with me, you can rest assured that I will work with them. And if that is so, then this troubled person stands a chance to one day help another troubled person, because that's the hope I see for us in this upside-down world.

In the rooms these days they say, "Don't quit before you get the miracle." Occasionally, the miracle doesn't sprout proper roots on the first planting.. Then maybe we need to dig a little deeper, change counselors, bring in another family member, find a way to bring the addict/alcoholic to a place of ruthless honesty; because the miracle is waiting just on the other side of the shame, begging to be released.

Now, I have been around a while. And I've seen thousands and thousands of sick men and women crawl out of hell storms like you don't want to know about. Like the one I crawled out of myself. But then, on the other hand, I've seen almost as many that maybe didn't seem quite as bad off who never "got it," and who may never "get it." And what's the difference? The ones that can't get it are wearing trousers that haven't been worn thin at the knee. That's the difference: the hold their addiction has on them prevents them from asking for help and accepting it. It's only a trip of maybe three feet, but for some it remains maybe the longest journey on Earth. I'm talking about men and women who are incapable of humbling themselves before a force that maybe defies rational understanding, that exists in a room called "faith." The door to that room is never locked, but you have to leave your cell phone and your pager and your calculator outside. You walk in there and maybe you light a candle or a stick of incense, maybe you pray in Russian or Swahili or Martian, for all I know. I don't care what words you use or who or what it is you address. In the end, you usually end up asking for help from the stars above and whatever it is that made them. But that's none of my business. My business is the trouble that got you there, and the trouble you can leave behind when you find a Higher Power, and realize through a relationship with this force that it's possible to forgive yourself for what seemed unforgivable. Because in that room called "faith," you learn to pull your socks up, and move on and up and through, and hopefully share a bit of your strength and hope at a meeting sometime soon. Without, that is, stressing the name you give to this Higher Power. All that's my business, and I'm still at it, getting the junk out and replacing it with understanding and love—my love, the Higher Power's, and the self-love of a soul out of trouble on that particular day who looks back on the hard work they've done and says, "I showed courage today. I took a step forward for myself and my family today. I fought the good fight, and just for this day, I'm as good as you can get at being straight and sober. I'm a winner!" If this person is smart and if we've taught him well, he'll hit his knees before he climbs into bed and thank his Higher Power for helping him be this winner on this day that has now come to an end. And when tomorrow's sun comes up over the hills, with no hangover, no blackout, no cigarette first thing out of bed, no pills thrown into the hopper first, no need to start the first sentence coming out of his or her mouth with the words, "I'm sorry," none of that, you start with a clean slate. That morning sun isn't an awful flashlight in your face anymore. No, it's a beautiful thing. And you realize all that trouble, hurt, and pain, truly was a gift.

About Villa Veritas

Villa Veritas Foundation, Inc., is a nonprofit organization dedicated to providing compassionate, interdisciplinary, chemical dependency treatment and ongoing educational programs. The Foundation's treatment philosophy addresses clients' physical, mental, and spiritual needs in accordance with the threefold disease concept of addiction. With more than fifty years of experience and excellence in their field, the Cusacks and their family of staff at Villa Veritas Foundation utilize the wisdom and healing of the Twelve-Step recovery model as their core principles and incorporate the most current technologies and techniques in their holistic approach. Their continued mission to assist people in finding recovery from addiction of all kinds opens the door to new opportunities for growth and success, new challenges, and renewed hope.